THE LOGIC AND
METHOD OF
MACROSOCIOLOGY

THE LOGIC AND METHOD OF MACROSOCIOLOGY

An Input–Output Approach to Organizational Networks

Krishnan Namboodiri
and
Ronald G. Corwin

Foreword by William Form

Westport, Connecticut
London

HM
490
.N75
1993

Library of Congress Cataloging-in-Publication Data

Namboodiri, N. Krishnan (Narayanan Krishnan).
  The logic and method of macrosociology : an input-output approach
to organizational networks / Krishnan Namboodiri and Ronald G.
Corwin ; foreword by William Form.
      p. cm.
  Includes bibliographical references and index.
  ISBN 0-275-94529-4 (alk. paper)
  1. Macrosociology. 2. Interorganizational relations. 3. Input-
output analysis. I. Corwin, Ronald G. II. Title.
HM24.N34 1993
301'.01—dc20   93-20302

British Library Cataloguing in Publication Data is available.

Library of Congress Catalog Card Number: 93-20302
ISBN: 0-275-94529-4

First published in 1993

Praeger Publishers, 88 Post Road West, Westport, CT 06881
An imprint of Greenwood Publishing Group, Inc.

Printed in the United States of America

(∞)™

The paper used in this book complies with the
Permanent Paper Standard issued by the National
Information Standards Organization (Z39.48—1984).

10 9 8 7 6 5 4 3 2 1

Contents

Figures and Tables

FIGURES

TABLES

Foreword

by William Form

The Logic and Method of Macrosociology represents the maturation of
sociology and a launching pad to realize the hopes of the discipline's
founders. A brief history of the field frames the basic problems that
Namboodiri and Corwin attack. From the perspectives of classical theorists, the title of this book might appear to be a redundancy because,
by definition, sociology, as the study of societies, was already macro.
Early efforts to study societies necessarily led to analyses of its components: institutions, communities, regions, and stratification systems.
These research targets still retained the macro perspectives of the discipline's founders. However, the later Americanization of sociology led
to a strange and unnecessary cleavage between social psychology and
social organization, with the former's emphasis on the individual gain-
ing ascendency even to the point of sometimes being equated to the
whole discipline.

How this devolution occurred cannot be documented here. Strangely,
the epistemological problem of how to cope with the individual and in-
dividuality were largely solved before World War II by the works of
Ellsworth Faris, George Herbert Mead, and others. Socialization and
social roles *in social organizations* were central axioms of their social
psychology, and the "individual behavior problem" was relegated to
clinical psychology. These lessons, however, were later ignored or distorted as they were "refined." Perhaps the spectacular growth of individual testing in psychology and the meteoric rise of classical economics
in American universities influenced the logic and methods of sociologists. "Behaviorism" and the "problem of action" remained central concerns of the field, and appeals to the "unity of the sciences" legitimized

the claim that individual behavior is the universal unit of all social sciences.

Equally important, before World War II, sociologists were known to be big on global ideas but soft in scientific methods, especially measurement. Sociologists first aped the methods and statistics of psychology and, later, those of economics. As Namboodiri and Corwin report, in both disciplines, individuals are the unit of analysis and are treated as if their behaviors are independent of each other. Sociology's central problems, as the authors clearly demonstrate, should deal with interorganizational relationships.

Yet, a century and a half after sociology was founded, the central problems of the discipline have not been consensually accepted. The fact that psychology and economics do not wrestle with interorganizational relationships still offers sociology the opportunity to expand into its historic niche, but the field's current fragmentation and its philosophical distractions may blind it to this opportunity. This volume shows how sociologists should proceed to enlarge their niche.

The previous sketch of sociology's main drift has ignored the efforts of a marginal minority to develop the discipline's core. Notably, before World War II, only human ecologists and some demographers insisted that the division of society's labor should be sociology's central concern. In their studies, interorganizational relations played a central function. Importantly, ecologists drew their theoretical inspiration, not from the behavioral sciences of psychology and economics, but from biology. In the 1950s, ecologists were joined by industrial sociologists who also insisted that, in an industrial society, sociology's main task was to study its complex organizations. Remarkably, from 1838, when August Compte coined the term "sociology," until 1960, empirical studies of interorganizational relationships were rare. After 1960, however, organizational sociologists became a stubborn, but growing, minority who adopted the mission to study "social structure." These self-labeled "structuralists" have defined the problems that should now dominate the discipline. The discipline's future depends on the ability of structuralists to convince their colleagues to work on the discipline's central problems. Although organizational sociologists have made considerable progress in this direction, Namboodiri and Corwin call for an attack on the general agenda with a comprehensive theoretical and methodological framework.

The authors have reviewed several approaches to the study of large-scale formal organizations as an interlocking set of suborganizations. They have also reviewed scholarly efforts to breathe life into formal organizations by studying the clique structures of their informal organizations. Finally, they have examined the methods currently used to study interpersonal and interorganizational networks, as well as those pertaining to organizational environments. Understandably, each area has its problems to resolve. Namboodiri and Corwin have confronted the challenge to develop a comprehensive theory and a method to attack the field's main problems within a single framework. Their input–output model permits the study of the *flow of activities through an interdependent system of organizations concerned with producing and distributing goods and services to consumer groups.* This approach considers the concomitant resolution of several problems: the micro-macro distinction, the internal–external organizational boundary problem, the organizational linkage problem, and structural versus change analysis.

A note of caution may help the reader absorb the lessons of this book. The illustrative chapters deal with two problems that, on the surface, appear to belong in the realm of economics, namely, earnings or income determination and the allocation of goods and services in society. In addition, the illustration of the full input–output framework in the final chapter is so densely mathematical that the untrained impatient reader may lose sight of its main message.

Chapter 5, Individualistic Theories of Earnings, summarizes the shortcomings of various theories that try to explain variations in individual earnings. To be sure, sociology has much to contribute to this task that has traditionally been the preserve of economists. But, as later chapters demonstrate, sociology's primary goal seeks to explain the *distribution of income* in society in terms of how its institutional organizations relate to each other. This task, of course, has been the traditional challenge of societal stratification, a field that many scholars claim occupies the very heartland of the discipline.

The final chapter on the input–output framework demonstrates how to examine relationships among organizations that are reciprocal, complex, and power-laden. This is illustrated by mathematically describing the patterns of interdependence among organizations that comprise industries, sectors, and regions. The sectors are then ranked in terms of their power or the impact that a given investment would have on the system. Direct and indirect effects on each sector are observed from each dollar's worth of increased demand compared to the output. This sounds complicated, and it is; but the social world is complex and sociologists must learn how to study and uncover its complexities, just as physicists have done in their area of study.

The advantages of the input–output framework are many, but three bear emphasis. First, the framework is straightforward and can be quickly understood; the mathematics to apply it are not beyond the capability of the coming generation of graduate students. Second, the framework can be easily adapted to other institutional arenas (e.g., education, health, and welfare). The challenge is the same: *to examine the flow of activities through the interdependent system of organizations concerned with distributing of educational, health, or welfare goods and services to various groups in the society.* Third, the comprehensive framework has both theoretical and applied applications. By changing the values in the flow of activities in any part of the system, the students can begin to understand how other parts of the interorganizational network are likely to change. The results of concrete government programs in the areas of health and education, for example, can be traced over time and applied to the framework to make it increasingly reflect the social reality. By adopting such an agenda, sociology indeed has a bright future.

Preface

In this book, we take the position that individual human beings are no more fundamental than the organizations that nurture and constrain them. In any analytic study, whether the topic is an individual, an organization, or something else, the subject matter can be represented only as a set of attributes. Dates, locations, and other identifying marks are attached to each attribute. The collection of such attributes, and relationships among them, then forms the basis for all synchronic and diachronic studies in the social sciences. The premise that, because an individual is more tangible than an organization, the former is more substantial than the latter is absolutely untenable. It amounts to saying that one set of attributes is more tangible than any other set. Naturally, organizations could not exist without people. However, from an analytic point of view, this only means that the aggregate properties of organizations include some human traits. The focus always is on aggregates of workers, consumers, and the like. Particular persons never enter into a scientific analysis. If human beings are no more fundamental than, nor different from, any other complex of statistical attributes, they require no special theories or methods. We do not subscribe to the position that explanations in the social sciences are incomplete until the investigator accounts for human motives. This tack would open an endless chain of factors ultimately leading to biochemical explanations. Every investigation must stop somewhere. That point is a matter of preference, not theoretical necessity. We prefer to stop with organizations, which are shaped by intricate and often elaborate relationships with still other organizations. In modern, developed societies, organizations have become numerous and complex. They are one of the most fundamental components of any society. It, therefore, seems self-evident that a central concern of sociology and related disciplines should be to describe and explain relationships among organizations.

Interest in organizational networks spans nearly half a century. In 1949, Philip Selznick published his seminal study of cooptation observed going on within the Tennessee Valley Authority. It was only one of myriad case studies produced during the post-World War II era, which were characteristically preoccupied with individual organizations. Yet, it was far more than just another case study of an organization because Selznick described, in detail, intricate relationships formed between the sponsoring agencies within the Federal bureaucracy and organizations in local communities responsible for carrying out the program.

In the early 1960s, several seminal papers introduced concepts and frameworks applicable to studying networks of organizations. Harold Guetzkow, Sol Levine and Paul E. White, and others advocated studying networks of organizations as they interacted with one another. One approach to this was to focus on a given organization and to trace its relationships to suppliers, monitoring agencies, and consumers of services and products. Another approach was to concentrate on global patterns of relationships within a total network without focusing on any particular organization (e.g., division of labor among member organizations).

The next decade yielded several significant studies in this genre, authored by Harrison White, Roland Warren, Herman Turk, Edward O. Laumann (and his associates), Kenneth Benson, and others, and culminating in 1979 with Howard Aldrich's landmark text and Joseph Galaskiewicz's study of exchange networks and community politics. During the 1980s, several important studies were published by David Knoke and James Kuklinski, Joseph Galaskiewicz and associates, and Ronald Burt, to mention a few. Some focused on phenomena associated with organizational networks, including interlocking directorates, resource dependency, and coalition formation. While the study of interorganizational relationships perhaps was not central to the field of sociology as a whole during these years, the literature was vital and insightful.

However, the promise of the 1980s was blunted by another development commencing during the mid-1970s. Inspired by several influential essays and studies, many productive sociologists swerved in another direction, splitting the field and dissipating some energy that might otherwise have been devoted to organizational networks. Michael Hannan and John Freeman, in particular; Howard Aldrich; Jeffrey Pfeffer; and others began promoting organizational ecology. It sparked much interest, an interest that perhaps to some degree has diluted the interorganizational focus in recent years. While Laumann, Knoke, Galaskiewicz, and others continued their work in the interorganizational tradition, Hannan and Freeman, Glenn R. Carroll, and several other sociologists were publishing numerous papers and books promoting this rival paradigm using sophisticated analytical techniques that could not be ignored. Their approach promised to correct at least two major deficiencies in the literature. First, it would deal with entire groups or populations of organizations rather than focusing on individual organizations. This new focus invited ecological perspectives which did enrich the field.

Second, it would give priority to the causal forces in the environment outside of organizations rather than assuming that they control their own destiny. This latter emphasis turned into a preoccupation of predicting organizational death rates from environmental conditions. The morbid focus obscured what we regard as a most important contribution of the ecology model, namely, to illuminate how *age structure* affects all kinds of transitions – changes in output, size, form, and control – many of which may be even more important than termination. Moreover, the fatalistic view of the environment, as the controlling force, caused researchers to neglect the *interplay* between internal control and environmental forces, which we believe is the fundamental dynamic that must be explained.

Despite substantial contributions and some promising moments, in comparison to the volume of publications throughout sociology and related disciplines, it seems fair to say that relationships among organizations have not had the central focus of social research in recent years. Even many sociologists who are interested in organizations per se (apart from the people in them) rely on theoretical and statistical models premised on the assumption that organizations exist independently of one another. For example, regression and related models in vogue presume that organizational structures and related explanatory variables are independent of one another. Organizational ecology, which has ascended into prominence in the last decade, also usually treats organizations themselves as populations of independent, unrelated objects connected only through presumed, and largely unmeasured, competitive relationships. An exception is that some attention has been given to simple interactions among populations of organizations analogous to the predator–prey relationships among animal populations.

Thus, today we have two parallel, independent streams of research: network analysis and organizational ecology. The social scientists who embrace network analysis are still vigorous and productive. However, the approach itself is fragmented by two disparate methodologies called structural equivalence and clique analysis. *Structural equivalence* is associated with the resource dependence approach. Organizational network models are said to be sophisticated extensions of it (Pfeffer, 1982). The other alternative, *clique analysis,* is sometimes called the graph theoretic approach (Laumann and Knoke, 1987). Both approaches have advantages and disadvantages, but they are antithetical. Thus,

according to structural equivalence, organizations must be grouped by
how they all relate to the same actors outside the set. This method of
defining a network does not consider how organizations relate to one
another within the set. On the other hand, the graph theory approach
(clique analysis) focuses on the reverse. It groups organizations based
on how organizations within a set relate to one another, regardless of
how they relate to outside actors. Both possibilities can be accommodated with the input–output model we develop throughout this book.

Social network analysis, as it is practiced today, is an extension of
an old technique called *sociometric analysis*. The purpose of sociometry
is to identify cohesive groups composed of individuals. Each person
provides information on their preferences and dislikes with respect to
other members of an identifiable group, such as co-workers in an office
or students in a classroom. These choices are then represented either
graphically or in matrix form. At first, social scientists analyzed such
data by performing simple, direct operations on the matrixes. This
could involve rearranging the rows and columns, or raising the matrix
to a power of two as a way of identifying mutual pairs. As large com-
puters became available during the 1970s, investigators employed increasing sophisticated and complex techniques. The so-called graph
theoretic applications became dominant in the post-1970 period. Alba
(1981) has traced this evolution from the 1940s forward. Block modeling and other clustering algorithms were introduced to delineate "positions" occupied by actors (see Alba, 1973). However, it is not clear that
these techniques have advanced knowledge of cliques very far. Reviewing this body of work, Borgotta and Kercher concluded that "the social
network analysis procedures do not generate easily interpretable results, and there is frequently the impression that intuitive analyses or
more rudimentary procedures are as effective as technical refinements"
(1988: 538).

The technical questions aside, we think too much attention is being
given to the internal linkages within networks, in comparison to their
consequences. In our opinion, research on organizational networks
stands to gain by focusing more intently on the input–output relationships within and between organizational networks. In the following
pages, we will describe and illustrate how to do this, using ideas first
developed in economics and then in regional science. The book starts
with an analysis of the micro perspective (Chapter 1) and proceeds to a
general discussion of the macro perspective (Chapter 2). Rival paradigms for analyzing organizations are reviewed in several chapters
that follow (Chapters 3 through 6). Analyses of interdependence among
organizations receive attention in Chapters 7 and 8. The latter is
devoted to an exposition demonstrating how input–output models can
be applied to organizational studies.

Both of us have been thinking about the ideas presented in the following pages for a long time. We have benefited immensely from the comments of various colleagues on earlier drafts of some chapters. In particular, we are grateful to Bill Form and Joan Huber, both of whom have been very generous with their time. We have also benefited from many of our students in graduate courses offered by the sociology department of the Ohio State University. We are intellectually indebted to numerous others whose names appear in the bibliography.

THE LOGIC AND
METHOD OF
MACROSOCIOLOGY

CHAPTER 1

The Limits of Microsociology: Are Individual Level Explanations Possible?

Macrosociology passes as a special area of sociology. Yet, it includes a wide spectrum of topics ranging from world systems to the political economy of nations, community and regional studies, and anlaysis of organizations. Therefore, we must ask ourselves, "What is distinctive about it?" We address this question in the following chapters. Our short answer is that macrosociology is concerned with the structures formed among interdependent sets of organizations that are most central to a society. We develop the position that interdependencies among organizations must be the focus of macrosociology. In subsequent chapters, we propose and use a systems approach to interorganizational network models. This approach can also address the questions central to organizational ecology. First, however, in this and the next chapter, we contemplate what the popular distinction between micro- and macrosociological approaches can and cannot mean.

One view of the discipline divides it into two discrete areas: microsociology and macrosociology. This belief gives the impression that macrosociology is the flip side of microsociology and, therefore, macro and micro approaches concern distinctly different types of subject matter. This way of looking at the discipline needlessly raises perplexing issues, such as:

- Is one part more fundamental than the other?
- How can the two parts be put back together, reconciled, or at least linked?
- Does each level require unique theories and novel methods of analysis?

We disagree with the basic proposition that there are two separate types of subject matter requiring different methods and theories that must be reconciled. We define *microsociology* as the study of selected attributes and behavior patterns associated with discrete members of a population of human beings. *Macrosociology*, as just stated, is concerned with structures formed among interdependent sets of organizations. The only difference is the unit of analysis involved. However, microsociology poses no unique problems and requires no special theories and methods. The need to reconcile theories about these two units is no more compelling than the need to reconcile any other two fields of sociology, such as research on the family and on nation-states. To develop these points, we start by considering what micro-level analysis is, and what it cannot be.

We shall see that microsociology is a broad umbrella covering diverse subjects. However, in this discussion we shall confine ourselves to what concerns us most, namely, the prevailing tendency to equate "micro" with a focus on individuals, who are presumed to be the most fundamental unit. Some sociologists consider sociological explanations barren unless they refer to individual human beings. We maintain, on the other hand, that sociology cannot study "individuals" if that term refers to unique human beings. Individual human beings are no more basic than organizations and other conceptual things. For scientific purposes, a person is also a conceptual thing, which loses distinctiveness during analysis. Moreover, when considered as unique personalities, individuals can never provide the basis of explanations. An explanation must rely on selected categories of characteristics shared by all individuals in the category. The logical explanatory structure used for microanalysis is not different from macro-level analysis. Therefore, one level cannot be more fundamental than the other.

We will consider in what sense individual level explanations are even possible. Our conclusion is that, despite what we often hear, an explanation can never grasp human beings as total personalities. Even emotions, thoughts, and similar psychological processes do not present any unique analysis problems that warrant special consideration. The only thing distinctive about individual level explanations is the set of variables one decides to include.

DEFINITIONAL AND THEORETICAL
REDUCTION DISTINGUISHED

The micro-macro distinction signifies discrete levels of analysis. It is, therefore, necessary to unravel contrasting meanings of "level" in this context.

Micro and Macro as Degrees of Importance

Writers subscribing to methodological individualism like to link micro and macro to degrees of importance. Only people and other things that take up space are real, according to this doctrine. Accordingly, only "real people" can actually make social events happen (Collins, 1981). If a person accepts that doctrine, then overt characteristics of a situation can be "explained" only as outcomes of individuals' activities (Watkins, 1953: 732; see Mayhew, 1980: 350; see also Mayhew, 1981). "Since individuals do all the acting," admonishes Hechter, "sociologists have to explain how it was possible to construct valid social theories without taking individual actors into account" (1983: 8). Consequently, Alexander adds, even macrosociologists must "ground their references to collective forces in the activities of observable, acting individuals" (1987: 13).

Speaking of a theory of action, Coleman proclaims the following:

The theory does not afford itself the luxury of beginning with already-formed units of social organization. Instead, it must begin with persons, and move up from there . . . , or it must be ultimately analyzable into relations among persons (1975: 85–86)

He declares, "Empirical research – particularly quantitative research – is largely concerned with explaining individual behavior" (1987: 153).

Reservations. Statements of this kind seriously misrepresent what takes place in the conduct of social research. There is nothing in the micro-macro distinction to suggest that things at the macro level can be reduced to more basic persona at the micro level without loss of explanatory power. Disputing that individuals are the ultimate elements, or "atoms," Simmel concluded a long time ago that all anyone can know about a person scientifically are single characteristics (1950: 6). For him, the individual is a synthesis of molecules, just as a river is a synthesis of particles of water. As large systems crystallize, he observed, they attain their own existence and laws.

Reduction Defined

The word "reduction" can mean two very different things, which are often confused.

Theoretical Reduction. Theoretical reduction is a technical term that refers to the relationship between parts and wholes. One can reduce something only by using theories based on properties making up its microstructure. That is not the type of reduction involved in individualism, since the theoretical composition laws of sociology are not logically derived from psychology.

Definitional Reduction. Several writers have tried to translate macro patterns into a different language using words that apply to individual behavior. However, the results do not qualify as theoretical reduction. They are best understood as definitional reduction. This only means that ultimately, every group-level concept is connected to individual behavior through hierarchies of defined terms. When something is true by definition, it is of no theoretical interest. While generalizations in the social sciences always presuppose intentional actions (Giddens, 1984), definitional reduction does not mean that humans are theoretically more fundamental than other constructs (Brodbeck, 1968: 297). Goffman observed that one cannot learn about the distribution of a city's land values by aggregating particular social encounters (1983: 9). He maintained that face-to-face behavior is no more real, nor any less of an arbitrary abstraction, than the dealings between two corporations.

WHAT IS AN INDIVIDUAL LEVEL EXPLANATION?

Aside from the fact that an individual is no more fundamental than any other social unit, a person cannot serve as the unit of analysis if "individual" is meant as a human being with an integrated, unique personality. To develop this point, we will need to reflect on what a so-called "individual level explanation" can possibly refer to. We see at least three different ways the term *individual* is being used in the literature. It can refer to

- *idiosyncratic qualities* of each discrete member of a population of human beings;
- *hypothetical thought processes* (e.g., calculation), motives (e.g., greed), intentions (e.g., to become a garbage collector), and emotions (e.g., fear) attributed by an investigator to a category of people; or
- *selected attributes* (e.g., age, gender) and *behavior patterns* (e.g., voting records) of discrete members of a population of human beings.

Individual-level variables in the first sense mentioned are impossible. In the second sense, they cannot add to an explanation if the mental processes are unverifiable, logical constructs. And, if in principle they are verifiable, they constitute no special issue (besides challenging measurement problems). Only in the last sense are individual-level explanations conceivable. Therefore, we define *microsociology* as the study of selected attributes and behavior patterns associated with discrete members of a population of human beings. The reasoning behind these conclusions is developed below.

The Idiosyncratic Meaning of Individual

All phenomena are individually unique. However, it is procedurally impossible to account for all such instances since empirical knowledge is abstract. Facts, as Weber noted, must be chosen selectively and organized through generalized, abstract categories (Parsons, 1947: 8). A causal law asserts only that any event having specified characteristics is accompanied by another event with specified characteristics (Hempel and Oppenheim, 1953: 326–327). The only necessary condition is repetition of the specified characteristics. It is impossible to consider all characteristics that make up an entity. Moreover, it is not necessary to predict specifically which individual instances do and do not fit the pattern. Yet, the impossibility of predicting individual behavior does not jeopardize scientific certainty. One can say with greater certainty that the religion of their fathers will be followed by a large group of persons than by a single person (Cohen, 1953: 671).

Consider the following proposition: "Children of rich parents go to college in greater proportion than do children of poor parents." As Lazarsfeld and Menzel (1961) point out, such a generalization asserts something about a set of elements (children) that are comparable in the sense that the same set of properties (i.e., wealth of parents, going to college) is used to describe them. Each element has a certain value on each property, which may be qualitative (going to college or not) or quantitative. The propositions assert relationships between the properties of the elements. It does not matter whether the elements are individual human beings or snowflakes, nor does it matter whether the properties are motives or weight. There is nothing special about individual-level theory construction. In no case can uniqueness be analyzed. We will return to this point later.

The Hypothetical Meaning of Individual

We sometimes hear that social phenomena cannot be understood without "taking the intentions and consequences of individual action into account" (Hechter, 1983: 8). Either intentions can be *observed*, or they are logical constructions discovered through *introspection*. The first method is verifiable; the second is not. If intentions are verifiable, they can be classified into categories and treated like any other attribute with no special problem (Ryle, 1949). On the other hand, if they are logical constructions, they are, in principle, unverifiable and outside the realm of scientific research (Beck, 1953; Nagel, 1953).

The most generous conclusion about the so-called "introspective method" is that it uses a special language to describe observations that can be described more effectively with the conventional language of science (Feigl, 1953: 624–625). H. B. English (cited by Turner) came to a less generous conclusion in his account of what he called the "ghostly tradition" of descriptive categories in psychology. Turner writes the following:

English attributed difficulties in the mind–body problem to the fact that psychological events and physiological events are abstractions of a fundamental process occurring in an anatomical locus. . . . One cannot explain how two constructions of the same process interact or how they reduce one to the other. The request for such explanations is apparently meaningless. (1965: 350–351; see also Mayhew, 1980: 345–346, 356; Webster, 1973: 272)

Efforts to discover how mental constructs interact with still higher levels of abstraction are equally meaningless. When people say they intuitively "understand" a connection, it means only that the interpretation being entertained is possible (see Abel, 1953: 685). It probably is not the only possible one. And, of course, not understanding something does not imply it is false. In fact, introspection can deceive anyone who confuses it with knowledge. Hempel and Oppenheim made the following observation:

The free fall of a physical body may well be said to be a more familiar phenomenon than the law of gravitation, by means of which it can be explained. . . . The behavior of psychotics . . . may sometimes be explainable and predictable in terms of general principles even though the scientist who establishes or applies those principles may not be able to understand his subjects (through empathy). . . . And . . . a strong feeling of empathy may exist even in cases where we completely misjudged a given personality. (1953: 330–331)

In sum, verifiable introspection poses no special problems, and as we demonstrate later, it requires no special methods. Unverifiable introspection can suggest hypotheses and restate empirical observations into other language. However, it does not add anything new to the explanation, and it carries risks of misleading the observer. To further illustrate these points, we next consider in greater detail the following cases: (1) mental constructs, (2) motivation, (3) the rational actor, and (4) historical interpretation.

Mental Processes as Intervening Connections. Introspection can be illustrated as follows (Abel, 1953: 679–680):

On a cold winter day, a man is seen carrying wood into his house. His neighbor wonders what he is up to, and considers several possible explanations, including these two: to get warm, or to burn down the house. Either interpretation could be correct, but from personal experience, the neighbor settles on the first possibility.

This explanation takes the following form:

1. Low temperature (A−) reduces the body temperature (B).
2. High temperature, or heat (A+), is produced by making a fire (C).
3. A person "feeling cold" (B′) will "seek warmth" by building a fire (C′).

The observer works with some facts and some speculations, which can be summarized symbolically as follows:

$$\text{Stimulus } S_1 \rightarrow \text{(Mental State A)} \rightarrow \text{Response R}$$
$$\text{Stimulus } S_2 \rightarrow \text{(Mental State B)} \rightarrow \text{Response R}$$
$$\text{Stimulus } S_3 \rightarrow \text{(Mental State B)} \rightarrow \text{Response R}$$

The preceding display illustrates that all we know for sure is a particular response (R), such as carrying firewood into the house. We also may know that one or more stimuli are present. In the illustration, we know it is cold (S_1); however, we may not be certain about other possible stimuli. For instance, perhaps the neighbor has recently gone bankrupt and wants to burn down the house to collect insurance (S_2). Or, perhaps the neighbor recently lost the house in a divorce settlement and plans to destroy it to prevent his wife from taking it (S_3). These stimuli, known and unknown, are associated with various mental states (represented by symbols A and B), which could intervene to produce the response (R).

Then, knowing one or more stimuli, how can we decide which of the two interviewing mental states is operating? Was the firewood meant to warm the house or to burn it down for some reason? The observer already knows that either is possible. The purpose of introspection is to speculate about which intervening process is most plausible, that is, more likely to be true. Any observer usually will choose whichever possibility occurs most frequently, a judgment based on the observer's experience. Specifically, the observer estimates the frequency of occasions on which neighbors use firewood to burn down their house relative to the occurrences when wood is used to heat a fireplace. Other factors may enter the final interpretation, such as whether the neighbor has a fireplace. The point is that the final interpretation is based on aggregate information. What one gains from introspection is nothing more than a reflection of the observer's knowledge (however imperfect) of the way categories of events are distributed. Introspection is simply an informed guess that a particular intervening connection is taking place, which is arrived at by imagining the emotions and motives that might be happening within the individual. There is no guarantee that introspection will improve the explanation. Improving it would require additional information about the person's behavior (e.g., habits and prior record of deviant acts).

Not included in this example are the unreported empirical events and connections that lead the observer to conclude that his neighbor was seeking warmth. Perhaps the intervening connection was not arrived at introspectively after all. Perhaps it was based on external clues, such as shivering, clothing worn, one's own body temperature, and the like. If so, introspection is not involved.

The Motivation Question. Apparently, one purpose of introspection is to discover motives. Some writers say that a relationship has not been explained until one understands what motivated it. This assumption is difficult to follow, however, because social causation occurs independently of individual motivations (Cohen, 1953: 671). Several examples come to mind:

- Overcrowding in cities does not intentionally spread diseases.
- Intending to help old people, the government increased Old Age Security Insurance benefits, which raised many elderly citizens to an income level that disqualified them for Medicaid (Sieber, 1981: 61; Zander, 1978: 66).
- A massive industry program to hire the unemployed in Detroit attracted job seekers to the city, increasing the unemployed ranks and contributing to riots (Banfield, 1974: 242; Sieber, 1981: 85).

Motives produce a predictable result only in the presence of other conditions, and, therefore, motivational analysis does not replace other types of explanations. When mental explanations are pursued exclusively, attention becomes fixed on one language system, precluding speculation on other grounds (Turner, 1965: 310). Thus, Boudon (1987) asks, why did the French agricultural system not develop as rapidly as the British system? Predisposed to look for motives, his answer turns on the ambitions of French landlords, who presumably left the land for more prestigious public offices. Another observer might, for example, stress changes in economic opportunities.

In the same vein, Coleman (1987) asks, why do people panic in an emergency? His answer is that each person independently makes a decision to do what everyone else is doing, that is, to transfer control of their own behavior over to others. This type of answer assumes that each person must independently decide. This assumption calls for psychological theories about each individual's perceptions of escape routes when the group's structure disintegrates. However, panic can also be seen as a response to the ratio of a population's size and number and location of available exits. Consider the following example:

Imagine a narrow bridge to which several roads lead. Automobiles reach the bridge from these roads. Since the bridge has only a single lane, the maximum density it can accommodate is one car at any given point on it at any given time. If two or more cars try to get on it simultaneously, both will fall into the river below. The characteristic features of the situation can be described in terms of the density that the bridge can accommodate, the time available for the cars to reach the other side of the bridge, the flow rate of cars reaching the entrance to the bridge from each feeding road, and so on. Once these parameters are fixed, the outcomes (i.e., the exit and accident rates) can be predicted. The whole exercise can be programmed on a computer without using psychological theories. The computer program can incorporate queuing to any desirable degree.

The Rational Actor. The idea that social phenomena are aggregate products of decisions made by individual actors requires no special methods of inference. The act of making a personal choice is an event defined by a transition from one state to another. If an individual decides to use birth control methods, for example, the transition is from not using contraceptives to using them. It is not unlike transitions from one job to another or, for a nation, from peace to war. The explanatory structure is the same. It is worth considering how other disciplines have approached the question of rationality.

Utility Models. One approach presumes that the decision maker maximizes *expected utility*. Utility theory is well developed and expounded in the economics literature (see, for example, Fishburn, 1983). This theory permits a technical definition of rational behavior — one that is clear and unambiguous, one that everyone can agree on. It stands in clear contrast with such vague definitions as "behavior based on reasoning." A utility model concerns mental calculations that are presumed to lead a decision maker to choose a unique course of action, under a given set of circumstances. The decision maker is pictured as perceiving several courses of action. Each action has certain perceived consequences carrying a certain subjective probability of occurrence and utility. The underlying assumption is that the action with maximum expected utility will be chosen over others. Since these mental processes cannot be observed, the model is a black box; that is, the inputs and outputs may be known, but internal workings are enigmatic.

It is useful to distinguish prescriptive models of decision making from descriptive ones. A model that presumes the actor will try to maximize utility is an example of a prescriptive model. It tells, for example, "how to gamble if you must." If one treats a utility model descriptively, it introduces a serious measurement problem because an element that usually is not measured directly enters the model. The way a decision maker perceives his or her actions and the likely outcomes must be inferred. Typically, these inferences are made from either the person's status characteristics (such as education) or their early socialization (see Easterlin, 1973). In either case, it is assumed that decision makers occupying a common location or sharing a history of transitions in the trait space will use a common preference structure.

Purposive Models. An entirely different approach is to think of rationality as a form of purposive behavior not unlike what occurs among subhuman forms of life, which are presumably incapable of reasoning. The adaptive behavior of simple biological organisms is purposive from the standpoint of some hypothetical goal toward which arrays of chemical, glandular, and sensory mechanisms are directed (Sommerhoff, 1950: 10, 23). A fly deliberately tries to escape when we try to kill it, but flies do not use rational thought processes in the usual sense.

Such behavior has been represented in mathematical models correlating characteristic behavior with critical environmental factors. Extrapolating such notions to human behavior, Sommerhoff observed the following:

Rational thought processes are, in general, neither necessary nor sufficient conditions for the occurrence of human behavior which is directly correlated to the agent's environment in precise objective sense of our definitions. (1950: 145)

If the purposive (goal-directed) character of life can be understood as a physical property of material systems, which can be represented mathematically, then we should not continue to attach importance to rationality as a necessary ingredient of explanatory frameworks of social phenomena.

Historical Interpretation. It is sometimes implied that historical explanations differ from other types of explanations. This is not so. Suppose one argues that a historical event (y), for example, India's independence from colonial status, can be explained via two historical factors: (a) change in parties that occurred in Great Britain after World War II, and (b) the leadership of Mohandas K. Gandhi. Three characteristics of this explanation can be noted:

1. Ignoring all other historical events, attention is drawn to an aggregate of hypothetical countries all of which have the segments (a) and (b) in common.
2. It is argued that (a) and (b) are only two of many plausible antecedents to y.
3. The association of (a) and (b) with y is a statement about the probability that, in this hypothetical universe, event y follows (a) and (b).

Notice the parallel between this and the interpretation made earlier about the neighbor collecting firewood.

The Attribute Meaning of Individual

Many supporters of microsociology are *philosophical realists,* or in other words, people who subscribe to the belief that the individual is more fundamental than other social units. Collins (1981) proclaims that an observer cannot see anything but encounters. Anything else has to be constructed. *Nominalists,* on the other hand, say that human beings are themselves reified constructs. They regard both psychological events and behavior events as abstractions of anatomical processes. They see human beings themselves as abstractions from chemical, biological, and emotional attributes. Taking this perspective, Berger, Eyre and Zelditch reject Collins's views. The micro world, they argue, is no less observer-constructed than the macro world (1989: 14).

Nominalism and Science. The only way to resolve perennial debates of this kind is on pragmatic grounds. From a pragmatic point of view, the scientific enterprise is more compatible with the nominalist's claims than the realist's position. The nominalist says an observer's understanding of something is always filtered by the categories used to think about it. One can never "point to" an object, only to selected attributes of it (Bergmann, 1957: 17). For example, when Mrs. A. points to her automobile, she may be directing us to look at its radiant paint, a flaw, or a cat within. "The meaning of a concept is determined, not by its pictorial connotations, but by the system of rules which implicitly defines that meaning" (Feigl, 1953: 623).

The nominalist's position describes exactly what is involved in scientific analysis: establishing categories of properties, classifying instances of objects, events, relationships, and the like associated with each category, and describing relationships between them. There is always selection in choosing the traits to be included and excluded. Nothing can be represented in its entirety, although the number of traits included can vary. In short, all forms of analysis rely on classifications of selected attributes in exactly the manner the nominalist describes the process of observation. This includes so-called individuals.

Individuals as Configurations of Attributes. As the reader has learned, the expression "individual-level" explanation can be misleading. Social scientists study only attributes abstracted from individuals, not the individuals themselves. We postulate that one can work only with configurations of properties of elements (Lazarsfeld and Menzel, 1961), and, accordingly, individuals never can be the unit of analysis. To develop this point, we

- treat human beings as distributions of attributes in attribute space,
- show that any analysis must be based on interchangeable aggregates,

- argue that there is no difference between so-called "categoric" and "individual" classes, and
- provide an illustration showing that there is no difference between analyzing mental states and any other property.

The postulate that one can work only with configurations of properties of elements is based on two features of modern analytic techniques: (1) an individual can be treated only as a configuration of selected attributes in an attribute space, and (2) individuals always are treated as distributions.

Blau defines *social structure* as a population distributed "among social positions along various lines—positions that affect people's role relations and social interaction" (1974: 616). There is considerable overlap between this definition and demographic analysis. Technically, demography is the systematic study of movements of people into, within, and out of a state space (social positions). A state space consists of an exhaustive list of combinations of ascribed and achieved characteristics of human individuals. For example, a person could be classified as one of the following:

- not married, not in the labor force;
- not married, in the labor force;
- married, not in the labor force; or
- married, in the labor force.

Each state is specified by combining (crossing) the distinction between *never married* and *ever married* with a distinction between *in* and *outside* the labor force. The analyst can introduce other distinctions as well (e.g., divorced, seeking work, and occupation). Depending on the type of population, entrance to the state space in question occurs via birth, immigration, and in-migration; exit occurs via death, emigration, or out-migration. To a demographer, a change in any major characteristic of a member of a population is an event. Transition from unemployed to employed is an event. Demography thus studies the probability that events will occur at specific durations after the occurrence of an earlier event (origin). Of particular interest is to determine how the events shape and reshape the size and composition of the human population involved.

Analysis of Human Aggregates. An analyst can refer only to aggregates of elements sharing a common configuration of selected properties. All elements in such an aggregate by assumption are substitutable among themselves. The principles described are no less applicable to human beings than to physical objects or corporations. When human individuals are involved, it doesn't matter whether the attributes of interest are mental states or social statuses. Uniqueness among elements within a class is never an issue. We shall pursue this line of reasoning in a moment.

Individuals as Points in State Space. Consider first how one might analyze the changing composition of an aggregate of human individuals. Each individual is represented by a point in a K-dimensional space. For example, if each individual is represented by values of three attributes, then that individual is represented by a point in a three-dimensional space. If the attributes are all measured on discrete scales, then each individual is an entry (a count of 1) in one of the cells of a K-dimensional table. In this latter case, all individuals in a given cell of the table are interchangeable (Lazarsfeld and Menzel, 1961).

What we usually think of as an individual is actually part of an aggregate. Viewed this way, the so-called micro-level analysis becomes structural analysis in the sense that Blau uses the term structural. The only difference is that he does not pay any attention to internal states of individuals, whereas the formulation just described imposes no such restriction.

"Categoric" and "Individual" Classes. To Goffman individuals identify each another in two ways (1983: 3). The *categoric* way involves placing the other in one or more social categories. The other way, the so-called *individual* way, locks the subject under observation to a uniquely distinguishing identity through appearance, tone of voice, and so on. However, the "individual kind" of classification is indistinguishable from the so-called "categoric kind." Think of a specific individual named John Jones. What is unique about him? To answer this question, we must enumerate relevant traits attributed to John Jones (and the values assigned to each). But then John Jones becomes described as a member of an aggregate consisting of objects sharing a particular combination of those features. John Jones ceases to be unique after all. He becomes substitutable with any other member of that aggregate.

Like it or not, *every sociologist dehumanizes human individuals by replacing each with vectors sequenced in time.* The vectors may consist of values representing occupation, education, income, marital status, rural-urban residence, and so on. They also may include values of mental states, such as ambition or depression. If we have measurements of these variables for each member of a population at successive points in time, it gives us a moving picture, showing how the distribution of people over this multidimensional space changes over time.

Mental States in Multidimensional Space. Does analysis of mental states differ in essential ways from other types of analyses? Sociology is about the distribution of attributes, not feelings and emotions. The modern literature on statistical analysis makes no distinction between variables that represent mental states and those that represent other states. The tabular view applies even when the attributes of interest are motives (e.g., greed) or emotions (e.g., hatred). Thus, no new principle is involved in treating a change from hatred to love as an event.

Consider the state called *empathy*. "Identifying" with someone intellectually or emotionally involves the following steps:

1. Each individual (*A* and *B*) is represented as a point in a *K*-dimensional space. Some of these dimensions presumably include mental states, such as anger.
2. Covariates of the variables in focus are determined.
3. We say congruence exists to the extent there is high correspondence between the value profiles of the two individuals on the focal variables.

The question then arises: How accurate is *A*'s identification with *B*? In other words, how far away from *B*'s actual location in the trait space does *A* place *B*? The distance between the actual location of a person in the trait space and the point where an empathizer places that person is a measure of accuracy in empathizing. The analyst can incorporate the distribution of such distance measures into a model of movement in the trait space. Consider the following example:

Suppose we are interested in whether a new tax policy has changed income inequality. In such an analysis, we are not interested in whether a particular individual has been helped, only whether the shape of the distribution has changed. Therefore, it is not necessary to know how particular individuals respond or how they feel about the policy.

THE DISTRIBUTION IS WHAT MATTERS

For a given population, there are *n* one-variable distributions of values in an *n-multidimensional space*. For example, there is a separate distribution for education, for occupation, for income, and for ethnicity (*n* = 4). In addition, there is a multivariate distribution for the total set of variables. In other words, there is a distribution consisting of every combination of values pertaining to the four variables just mentioned. This distribution can be created by arraying combinations of the four variables as rows and as columns in a table. In addition, there are distributions for the marginals of the table. Each individual is represented somewhere on each of these distributions. The distribution of responses is what matters.

Individuals in Statistical Models

Think for a moment about what happens when individuals are entered into statistical models commonly employed in sociology.

Regression Equations. First, consider a regression relationship in which all data points are for individuals. An example is the relationship between the so-called "drive to get ahead" (call it Y) and strength of commitment to Protestantism (call it X). Assume for the moment that both variables are measured on continuous scales. Now think of a regression relation of the type: $Y = a + bX + e$. The relationship seems to be between two attributes of individuals; it is not, though, for the error term introduces a distribution. In fact, what it says is the following: (1) Individuals with a given value for X, for example, X', (2) considered as an aggregate (3) have a distribution of Y whose mean is $a + bX$.

The Discriminant Function Approach to Classification. Return for a moment to the observer Abel described earlier in our illustration of the person who witnessed his neighbor bringing wood into the house. The story is not about an "in-the-flesh person" whose identity is shaped by details of anatomy, psychological makeup, social background, climate, and a myriad other things. The incident is not even about two hypothetical individuals. It is about two classes of entities:

1. A class of hypothetical "observers" who share certain specified traits with the observer in the story; the members of this class vary in many unspecified respects.
2. A class of hypothetical "wood gatherers" who share certain unspecified characteristics with the wood gatherer in the story; the members of this class also vary in many unspecified respects.

The question Abel (the analyst) asks is about classifications. His guess is that most observers would place most wood gatherers in the class "gathered firewood to light a fire in the fireplace." He also infers that very few observers would place more than a few wood gatherers in the class "gathered firewood to burn down house."

Here is the point of that story then: Such interpretations are all about putting things into classes. To perform this type of exercise, each class is defined as a hypothetical collection of objects whose members share a specified set of properties. It is this notion that is formalized in discriminant function statistical techniques developed (beginning with Fisher, 1936) for classification work. This form of inference approaches explanation by classifying an object from information to date and considering differential costs of wrong classification. In the two-group case, the problem of classification is to decide to which of the two groups a given object belongs. The following is an example of calculating the probability of misclassification:

Suppose a decision to classify an object has to be based on one measured variable (X). Suppose this variable is normally distributed both in class I and class II. There is a common standard deviation (s), and the means are m_1 and m_2, respectively. The value of X for a new object is known, and the task is to put the object into the correct class. If $m_1 < m_2$, we may follow the rule that the object is to be assigned to class I, provided X is less than halfway between m_1 and m_2. Otherwise, it is to be assigned to class II. It is easy to show that, if this rule is followed, the probability of misclassification of an object from a given class is 0.5 (d/s), where $d = m_2 - m_1$.

For some classifications, it is known from experience that objects come more frequently from one class than another. (People use firewood more frequently for the fire in the fireplace than to burn their house down.) Also, misclassifying an object that comes from one class may have more serious consequences than misclassifying an object from the other. If these relative frequencies and relative costs are known, the boundary point can be shifted to a value that minimizes the average cost of a mistake in repeated trials.

Many features highlighted in this illustration are fundamental in the so-called micro-level interaction. People guess the intent and purpose of an act and classify it accordingly. Then, they react to the consequences associated with the class they have chosen. Every time, people are putting each other into categories. They are, in short, dealing with aggregates.

WHAT IS PROBLEMATIC ABOUT LINKING LEVELS OF ANALYSIS?

Many writers are worried about how to link micro- and macro-levels of analysis. A similar issue is being successfully addressed in other literature, two of which we will mention.

Multilevel Analysis

There is a voluminous literature on multilevel analysis addressing questions such as why is income inequality different in two or more societies? The approach involves the following two steps (see, for example, Bock, 1989; Wong and Mason, 1985; Mason, Wong, and Entwisle, 1983; Hermalin and Mason, 1980).

A Simplified Model. *Step 1.* A model is fitted for data collected for units at one level, separately in each of several contexts. An example is the regression equation:

$$Y = b_0 + b_1X_1 + b_2X_2 + e$$

fitted separately for each of five countries using data on Y, X_1, and X_2 collected in a cross-national sample survey of individuals. Here, countries are the contexts, and the original observations are obtained at the individual level.

Step 2. If estimates of a coefficient (X_1, for example) vary by countries, one tries to account for the variation in terms of country-level variables. This may involve, for example, fitting regression equations of the following type:

$$b_1 = h_0 + h_1G_1 + h_2G_2 + e'$$

Notice that in this approach, one completes the explanation by going to more inclusive levels in the nested hierarchy rather than reducing one level to another. The strategy is dictated by the nature of the question asked. Why does the effect of X_1 on Y vary between countries?

Logically this approach is equivalent to what sometimes is called "contextual explanation" of patterns within a distribution of human individuals in a multidimensional space consisting of structural parameters (education, income, occupation, etc.).

Linking Levels through Multidimensional Space. The notion of multidimensional space described above is a general approach that applies to the composition and mobility of populations of families, or of labor unions, corporations, nations, and so on. Instead of human individuals, suppose we think about so-called "families." Assume that we can enumerate all relevant features of families. Then, we could think of a multidimensional space to represent families described in terms of the characteristics of interest. For purposes of easy reference and to distinguish it from the multidimensional space for human individuals, let us call this the family space. Again, we can study the compositional shift of this population, its determinants, and consequences.

We may be interested in linking the structure and dynamics of such a population to the structure and dynamics of a population of individuals. For example, the formation of husband–wife pairs can be linked to the changing distribution of human individuals in their multidimensional space. Similarly, we can link the breakup of marriages to the structure and change in the population of individuals. For example, we may entertain the possibility that A and B are more likely to marry if they have certain features than if they have certain other features. The same is true for divorce, separation, and the like, having the nth child, and so on.

While the solutions illustrated are incomplete, we think the problematic aspects associated with linking individuals' attributes to attributes of units at other levels of abstraction have been exaggerated.

Why Linkage?

The question is: "What are the advantages of doing so?" In the discipline of economics controversies over micro-macro levels of analysis have been going on for some time. Economists committed to methodological individualism maintain national income is nothing more than a summation of individual incomes. This school believes that even when the initiating forces are instituted by a national program, nothing really happens until individual persons make microeconomic decisions.

We fail to see why it is essential to know how the macro stimuli are translated into microdecisions. It is enough to assume that microdecisions will be made to produce a distribution of outcomes. It does not make any difference who happens to fall in which end of the distribution or who is in the middle. What matters is that a distribution of outcomes follows the introduction of the macro forces.

SUMMARY AND CONCLUSIONS

As background for the macro approach taken in this book, this chapter has addressed some beliefs about micro versus macro levels of analysis. Claims to the contrary aside, we conclude that microanalysis is no more fundamental than any other type of sociological explanation. Individual human beings are abstractions, and, therefore, they can never be treated as total personalities. Hypothetical individuals are no more real or concrete than any other level of abstraction. Exactly comparable to any other unit of analysis, individuals are always members of select, abstract categories and thus must be treated as constellations of attributes. Accordingly, we defined microsociology as the study of selected attributes and behavior patterns associated with discrete members of a population of human beings.

A micro-level thing is not a naturally occurring attribute. The smallest unit in any schema is called micro. Therefore, the term has no identifiable properties that are inherently problematic, apart from those associated with any part–whole relationship. If so, the distinction between micro and macro levels of analysis adds little to the existing literature on the substantive properties of collectives and members.

Explanations using individual-level properties present no special problems, because all explanations use the same inference structure.

Figure 1.1
The Black Box Explanatory Model

Context   —»   [**Means-to-ends**   ]   — »   **Distributions**
                                  Calculations   **in State Space**

Even *verifiable* forms of introspection can be analyzed with existing methods of compositional and transitional analysis (if the thought processes involved can be reliably measured). An introspective decision to seek a new job has the same structure as the transition of an organization from ten to twenty departments. *Unverifiable* introspection is special but outside the canons of proof and, therefore, is not relevant to the social sciences.

The reductionistic position is ultimately self-defeating because it logically forces the analyst to adopt a biochemical explanation of human behavior. Social sciences other than sociology are better prepared for this task. Anyone who is determined to go into the details will find an endless amount of them concerning a particular decision. For example, deciding to have an abortion can involve the woman's friends and relatives, finances, medical history, and so on. No one, not even the most zealous advocates of rational choice, ever collects data on all the complex details implicit in this approach. Invariably, some levels and sequences are left unspecified.

Consider the way we usually explain other life situations:

It is generally known there is a high positive correlation between the mileage on a car and the probability that it will break down. We act accordingly by routinely trading in high-mileage cars. Presumably the relationship has something to do with manufacturing technology, metal fatigue, quality controls during production, durability of materials, and the like. The engineers responsible for designing the product may need to know these details, but most of us do not need to understand the engineering principles involved, only the relationship. Cars wear out with repeated use.

Each unspecified segment of an explanation is a "black box" within the model (Figure 1.1). Using black boxes is not qualitatively different from the way in which many analysts treat the entire means-to-end calculations of human individuals (e.g., Blau, 1974; Hawley, 1986). A black box sets aside the context so the analyst can focus on relationships between context and the distributions in the state space without getting lost in the morass of individual decision making.

We are not saying one should never be interested in what is going on inside the metaphorical box. What we are saying is that, in many practical situations, it is justifiable to ignore the intervening processes. Any other position commits us to the impossible task of trying to account for endless sequences of intervening variables. Incompleteness is inherent to the analytic process.

In sum, including individual properties in an explanation does not make it more thorough than any other type of explanation. It is not necessary to predict the behavior of particular individuals. What matters is how selected characteristics are *distributed*.

CHAPTER 2

In Search of Macrosociology

We said that the micro level pertains to selected attributes and behavior patterns of discrete members of a population of human beings. Implicitly, they are the smallest social unit. Where, then, is the macro level? That question is addressed in this chapter.

WHERE IS THE MACRO LEVEL?

As commonly employed, the term "macro level" covers any residual part of society not attached to individual human beings. This leaves much to the imagination. On the face of it, the term is so broad and ambiguous that it seems to have no specific referent. However, a group of sociologists have gone to the other extreme to claim it for one topic — the study of nation-states in the world economy. We believe the idea is broader than that. If a nation-state is the only macro unit, then shall we regard organizational ecology, stratification, the economy and other institutions as "micro" topics? Many other units should be included, such as regions within a nation, populations of organizations, and social institutions, to mention a few.

There is no point quibbling over a word, except in this case, where the word sets the focus and direction of the discipline. The loose dichotomy between micro- and macrosociology is troublesome because it provides no consistent focus. The notion encompasses nearly everything left over beyond the individual — from families and organizations to communities, regions, and nations. Is one unit inherently more macro? Do they have something in common? We find two answers — one logical and the other strategic — which are not mutually exclusive. Taken together, they provide alternative ways to define macrosociology.

First, from a logical standpoint, the micro-macro distinction refers to a relationship between a whole and its parts. The term macro stands for a relationship, not a particular social unit. Something micro is a component of a more abstract unit. This usage avoids the dilemmas of permanently binding macro to a specific unit, whether nations, organizations, or individuals. Since some units are more abstract than others, whatever one chooses to study, it can be broken down into its micro components. We recognize that, because world systems encompass a wider range of social units than, say, communities, some people prefer to associate that topic with macrosociology. However, we are inclined to take another approach.

The second tack approaches the issue from a strategic standpoint. We have singled out the organizational network as a particular instance of the whole–part relationship. As we see it, all macro-level phenomena have one thing in common: they can be accounted for by networks of organizations. When one thinks of a nation, a region within it, or a region of the world, they all comprise organizations. Therefore, in our opinion, organizational networks are the critical ingredient of macrosociology. The purpose of this chapter is to sharpen this organizational focus.

Types of Collectives

In a neglected paper, Lazarsfeld and Menzel (1961) resolved the residual character of the distinction in the first way. They succeeded in classifying analytic relationships between a whole and its parts without reference to the obscure micro-macro terminology. Distinguishing between collectives and members, they defined a *collective* as an entity composed of parts. Then, *members* who make up a collective are components with comparable characteristics. It is important to remember that members of collectives are not necessarily human beings. They can be gangs, families, cities, businesses, and so on. What is most significant about collectives is that they can be understood without reference to their individual members.

Lazarsfeld and Menzel identified four types of member properties and three types of collective properties. See Figure 2.1 for examples of each.

Properties of Members:

1. *Absolute properties* are attributes belonging to members.
2. *Relational properties* are computed from information about the observable relationships between members.
3. *Comparative properties* relate a member to a distribution.
4. *Contextual properties* describe a member by properties of a collective.

Properties of Collectives:

1. *Analytic properties* are obtained by performing some mathematical operation on properties of the members.
2. *Structural properties* are obtained by performing some operation on data about relations among the members.
3. *Global properties* are integral attributes of collectives not based on information about the individual members.

Here are some other principles underlying this typology:

- Individual human beings can never be treated as total personalities but only as classes of attributes shared with other members.
- Relationships are meaningful units of analysis apart from specific actors and the content of their interactions.
- Any property may be treated as problematic in one analysis and taken as given in another, thus allowing one to focus on something else.
- Any unit, including individual human beings, may be regarded as collective in one context and a component in another.

Figure 2.1
Types of Members and Collectives

PROPERTIES	EXAMPLES
Absolute	A person's psychological characteristics, behaviors, and status characteristics; an organization's name, location, and size.
Relational	Discussions between supervisors and workers; balance of trade between two nations.
Comparative	Sibling order; a city's rating in the bond market.
Contextual	Graduates of College X are politically conservative; teachers who opposed a work stoppage when the community had no industries to tax decided to go out on strike when a large factory moved in.
Analytic	The mean age of nurses in a hospital; the proportion of all grocery stores ending in bankruptcy.
Structural	Mean rates of interaction among members of two friendship cliques; the correlation between meetings among a hospital federation and costs of medical care.
Global	The presence of time clocks in a factory; the number of departments in a corporation; the proportion of a national budget allotted to education.

Levels of Sampling Units

The precept that members of a collective are not necessarily individual persons (Lazarsfeld and Menzel, 1961: 424) opens the door to a second order of macro-level properties—a hierarchy of sampling units. There are five types of units that can be sampled:

1. *Individual human beings* (e.g., selected attributes summarized in such a way that people lose their identities), including:

   - Psychological states (e.g., motives and attitudes, thoughts and emotions),
   - Behavior patterns (e.g., attendance record), and
   - Status characteristics (e.g., age, sex, gender, social status).

2. *Organized groups* (e.g., play groups, gangs, families).
3. *Formal organizations* (e.g., hospitals, corporations, government agencies).
4. *Clusters of organizations* (e.g., hospital federations, United Nations, interlocking boards of directors).
5. *Geographical units* (e.g., cities, school districts, counties, regions, states, and nations).

Aggregates and Units

Any sampling unit can be treated either as an *aggregate* or as a *unit* (or more precisely, an entity with a unit character). Elements of aggregates are interchangeable and independent of one another, related only "definitionally" through classification criteria. Members of units, on the other hand, are differentiated among themselves and interdependent. Reflecting on the relationship between sampling units and properties of collectivities, one can see that

- frequency counts of individuals (i.e., censuses) typically yield only aggregate data;
- structural relationships can represent only collectivities;
- thoughts and emotions pertain only to people;
- integral properties can belong only to collectivities; and
- behavior, status characteristics, relationships and contextual properties may pertain to any sampling unit.

MACROSOCIOLOGY DEFINED

It is commonly acknowledged that organizations are the core subject matter of sociology (Hawley, 1992; Coleman, 1975; Namboodiri, 1988; Laumann and Knoke, 1987: 8). Parsons (1960) saw them as the primary mechanisms for carrying out societal objectives. In addition, they have figured prominently in theories of social stratification based on how power is distributed and exercised in society. Karl Marx (1954) was acutely aware of the social inequities resulting from a concentration of power in economic organizations. Today, the most powerful elites and veto groups obtain power because they represent coalitions of organizations. The importance of these organizational networks has eclipsed the simpler bureaucracies that concerned Weber. In sum, differences among organizations should account for outcomes for any unit above characteristics of individuals or aggregates of them.

With this in mind, we define *macrosociology* as the systematic study of the unitary collective properties of organizations and organizational networks. This usage comes close to what many regard as the core of sociology (cf. Namboodiri, 1988: 622). Note the following:

- Our definition avoids equating studies of geographical units with macro sociology. Nations, regions, cities, and the like are the contexts in which organizations and networks function and thus can be accounted for in terms of organizations comprising them.
- Since families share properties of individual persons with those of formal organizations, they can be regarded as organized groups, which are marginal but, nonetheless, relevant to the interests to macrosociology.
- Aggregates (i.e., status categories, such as being male) have been excluded from this definition; they are central to demography but of interest to macrosociology, as we are using the term, only to the extent they are in the process of becoming units.

THE IRONY OF MACROSOCIOLOGY

Since most social life transpires in organizations, differences among organizations should account for outcomes at the macro level, that is, any unit except human traits or aggregates of them. Organizations should be sampled and used as the unit of analysis. We, therefore, find it ironic that they have been nearly totally ignored in precisely the literatures where, logically and empirically, they are most relevant. To illustrate our point, consider for a moment research in several areas that are commonly considered to be macrosociology.

Social Structure and Intermarriage

During the past decade, Blau and associates (1984) have been working on a macro theory of intermarriage based on the premise that size distribution and heterogeneity of groups affect their members' chances of marrying outside their group. One theorem is:

In-group norms against intermarriage are less potent than the size of the group and the number of different groups in contact in determining whether inter-marriage will occur.

Being part of a small group in heterogeneous communities increases the probability that chance meetings will occur among persons from different backgrounds. These contacts, in turn, foster intermarriage. The source of data is married couples in counties located in metropoli-tan areas. The authors of the study found that

The greater an SMSA's [Standard Metropolitan Statistical Area] heterogeneity in national origin, mother tongue, ethnic background, region of birth, industry, and detailed occupation, the more likely it is that young married couples differ in these respects. (Blau and Schwartz, 1984: 56)

Since racial heterogeneity was not correlated with intermarriage until socioeconomic status was controlled, the researchers concluded that income differences suppress racial intermarriage.

Reservations. Notice that the so-called "groups" in question are not interacting units. They are aggregate categories made up of individuals with similar status characteristics. Furthermore, the model itself strongly resembles the "marriage squeeze" phenomena commonly dis-cussed by demographers. We see little difference between predicting marriage rates from disproportionate sex ratios and from dispropor-tionate ratios of racial and ethnic groups.

Neither the marriage squeeze approach nor Blau's model addresses why heterogeneity should lead to positive interaction rather than to segregation. We suggest that those outcomes depend on the composi-tion and distribution of various types of organizations making up any community. An imbalance of black and white youths may not promote interracial marriage if both races work in different places and never at-tend the same night clubs, churches, colleges, schools, and classrooms.

Why Organizations Should Be the Focus. We will learn far more about intermarriage when researchers start paying more attention to the distribution of organizational settings where, we know, "chance meetings" take place in metropolitan areas. They include work places, schools, colleges, churches, restaurants, bars, parks, political organiza-tions, and other voluntary organizations where young people go. When labor markets, residential neighborhoods, and the like are segregated, it will impede interracial marriage. Some organizations draw clientele exclusively from neighborhoods; others are cosmopolitan. The distri-bution of different types of jobs (e.g., white collar, construction, etc.) and types of work organizations affects employers' inclinations to hire from one or more ethnic groups.

If the mix of organizations in a community is a crucial determinant of marriage opportunities, as we maintain, then it is important to ask questions such as the following:

- What is the mix of work places drawing on heterogeneous and relatively homogeneous backgrounds?
- How segregated are the schools and churches?
- What proportion of restaurants draw customers citywide, and how many draw customers from specific neighborhoods?
- What proportion of marriage partners meet outside their own communities through work-related travel and extended friendship and family groups?

In other words, if the prime locus of macro events is in organizations, then organizations should be the main units of analysis.

Organizational Capacity and Conflict

Scholars have customarily attributed work stoppages to the business cycle and politics. However, in the 1970s investigations in several nations demonstrated that organizational structures are equally important sources of industrial conflict. It has been convincingly argued that strikes depend upon:

- the ability of workers to organize and form large unions (Britt and Galle, 1972; Shorter and Tilly, 1974).
- the likelihood that an organized work group can generate widespread economic disruption (Perrone, 1984).
- the power of organized employers and government agencies to suppress walkouts (Sndyer and Tilly, 1972; Griffin, Wallace, and Rubin, 1986).
- the threat of third-party interventions that could change the balance of power.
- the permissiveness that authorities show toward minor acts of defiance in the early stages of labor unrest (Cole, 1967: 129; Lammers, 1969).

Reservations. Despite a growing awareness of the critical role organizations play in social conflict, researchers sometimes overlook them or confuse them with related, yet less significant, structural forms. For example, Perrone (1984) set out to demonstrate that even small groups like garbage collectors can be powerful when they perform essential services. Unfortunately, his measure of this kind of "positional power" was based on aggregate measures at the level of entire industries, not the work organizations where strikes occur. As Wright (1984) noted, no matter how many people depend on a group's services, it cannot strike without a strong union or comparable organizational power base. Here, then, is another instance where a promising attack on macro-level issues got off the track because the researcher overlooked the organizational locus of the events of interest.

The World Systems Literature

What puzzles us the most is the disregard for organizations one sees in the burgeoning research on world systems. It is, after all, the very literature that is supposed to be most dedicated to macro, structural forms of analysis; yet, due to two proclivities in the writing, organizations are seldom mentioned by name. First, authors rely heavily on psychological concepts to interpret macro events; and second, they use vague euphemisms, which only serve to obscure the organizational settings involved.

Psychological Bias. Two phenomena that have been conspicuously mentioned are rural-to-urban migration and violence. Authors frequently try to account for such trends in psychological terms, such as "perceived opportunities," "rising expectations," "relative deprivation," and the like (see, for example, Bradshaw, 1987: 226). Yet, there is a better way to explain violence and migration. Both are products of uneven patterns of change among key organizations. For example, when schools prepare workers for office jobs that do not exist, they will be inclined to look elsewhere for work; or they may unite and take collective action, which, in turn, requires an organizational structure to coordinate desperate activities. Some sociologists (e.g., Huntington, 1968; Zimmerman, 1980) have suggested that social problems arise when the kind of status that is associated with increasing levels of literacy and education changes at a faster rate than the kind of status associated with occupational structure (skilled and white collar jobs) and political structure (e.g., elections).

Euphemisms. The world systems literature contains an annoying fondness for euphemisms, such as "political consciousness," "political participation," "elite unity," and "urbanization." The term "dependency" itself is shorthand for specific organizational actors and, so, falls in the same category.

Political Consciousness. We hear, for example, that violence is precipitated by something called "political consciousness." However, some writers attribute the cause to "education" (see, for example, Delacroix and Ragin, 1978). Sometimes these two words are used interchangeably. Consider first political consciousness. It has behavioral referents, such as forming political parties, attending political rallies, organizing protests, and registering voters. Every one of these actions requires organizations.

Where does political consciousness come from? Granted, some of it may spring from the exasperation individuals feel after watching too much television. However, there must be much more than that behind new political organizations. One possibility is connections with political parties in other nations. Others that come to mind are the influence of immigrants, or of tourists, and contacts some citizens may have with colleges as they study and travel abroad. Whatever the actual details, we suggest looking carefully at the organizations people belong to.

Some writers attribute political activism to education. It is a good bet that political consciousness is aroused by something that happens in schools. However, we know that formal education (expressed simply as number of years of schooling) cannot be the answer. Why should simply being in a school make people into political activists who are ready to undertake violence? Students usually do not learn only to be politically liberal and violent. There is extensive literature accusing schools in the United States of a conservative bias — of turning out obedient workers for industry anxious to conform to the bureaucratic work ethic.

The outcomes of schooling, whether violence or conformity, depend on many things. It is necessary to find out who teaches whom, what they teach, the social composition of different schools, the distribution of different types of schools throughout a nation, the ties among them, and their relationships with the state and other sources of power.

It would be important to identify different types of schools and then find out how they are distributed between urban and rural areas, who attends them, and, especially, who controls them. Are they decentralized and controlled by neighborhoods or churches, or are they controlled by the central government? The number and distribution of schools, and their control structure, we suggest, will account for a significant part of the variance in peaceful political activity as well as violence. Again, what we are saying is that focus should be on the organizations where political consciousness is nurtured.

Political Participation. Political participation is another popular, but vacuous, term. It seems to suggest that political parties and interest groups are being formed within a nation. Again, these organizational referents are obscured by the language. It would be important to know how many parties exist, what proportion of the population belongs to them, and their relationships to one another and to the government.

Elite Unity. The charge is often made that "dependent development empowers an upper class of landlords, comprador bourgeoisie, and transnational corporate manager" (Boswell and Dixon, 1990: 543). This might be true, but that is a diverse bunch of people. What unifies them? How do we know that elites from such different backgrounds share the same interests? If there is such a class, the diverse groups involved would have to have some means of communicating, planning, and taking concerted actions. In other words, members of the class must be connected by networks of organizations.

It is, of course, possible that such organizational networks do not exist and, therefore, power is not as structured as certain theorists believe. Some writers contend that disunity is the "generic condition of national elites" (Higley and Burton, 1989: 20). Whatever the answer, the issue turns on the presence or absence of the necessary organizational structures.

Urbanization. The concept, urbanization, is often introduced into discussions of modernization, and treated as though it were some kind of independent force for change. That is misleading because urbanization is a residual category – a blanket term. It covers population distribution, demographic composition, ecological characteristics, and, especially, organizational capacity.

The fates of urban places depend upon the organizations that comprise them. For example, a city's economic and political power partly depends on the number and types of big corporations and national headquarters located within it (Turk, 1977). The economies of cities in the Sunbelt have improved as large corporations have moved their headquarters to that section of the country (Palmer and Friedland, 1987: 146).

The density of this organizational base is not uniform across all cities. Therefore, it is necessary to dig beneath the superficial indicators of urbanization to find the frequencies and distributions of different organizations that might be involved in events of interest in the evolution of world systems.

Dependency. Even the central concept, economic dependency, is an abbreviation which sometimes does more to obscure the underlying organizational structures that link nations to one another than to clarify. Consider a measurement that is commonly used: foreign investment measured in dollars. Investments could be in the form of loans from banks to local businesses or to foreign investors who, in turn, purchase foreign technology from factories around the world. Investments also reflect penetration by multinational corporations. Multinationals, in turn, sometimes buy up existing extracting industries or manufacturing plants, but they also might start new factories. Often, these corporations have enough power to obtain significant tax concessions, but when the government is strong, they may be forced to negotiate unfavorable terms. Thus, we would need to know about the power of the corporations involved, the strength of local governments, and whether some governments have policies that help protect local industry.

Implications. When findings do not occur as predicted, researchers are sometimes forced to reconsider the implicit organizational basis of their theories. For example, puzzled by a positive relationship between economic development and rebellions, Boswell and Dixon speculate that maybe developed nations have better communication networks and stronger unions and other types of organizations (1990: 554). That would seem obvious. Why not take into account union strength, number and representation of political parties, church activities, and other indicators of organizational capacity in the first place? Also, notwithstanding the insistence of Marxists, too little attention is being given to factories themselves as arenas of political turmoil and conflict. Their size, composition, and distribution would be worth considering (for a notable exception, see Jenkins, 1983).

In any event, it is clear that economic development is a function of infrastructure within a nation and how that structure relates to other nations. To account for the direction and pace of national development, at a minimum, one must understand the following:

- How economic sectors and job markets are organized
- The power relations between government agencies, courts, and repressive bodies such as the military
- Laws supporting and inhibiting organized labor
- Ties between business elites and schools and colleges

INPUT–OUTPUT MODELS

Perhaps we have said enough to make the point that the very researchers who are devoted to purportedly macro-level issues, often overlook the pivotal importance of organizations, even when they play a crucial role in the issues being addressed.

The Role of Organizations

The social units we customarily call a social system, a nation, a region, a market, an industry, and the like are basically composed of networks of organizations. For example, as Leifer and White (1987) argue, producers gauge the demand for their products from the performance of competitors. This aspect of a market, they are saying, is a product of relationships among competitors. Turning to another example, there is evidence that when establishments are faced with severe market constraints, they enter mergers and their directors form ties. This says that through such relationships, business organizations increase their leverage over market performance (see Burt, Christman, and Kilburn, 1980). The other side of the equation is how they are tied to important actors at the national level, such as the boards and Federal agencies that control the stock market exchanges here and abroad. One cannot understand markets apart from the networks of organizations that operate them.

Underlying Assumptions

The input–output model is suitable to tackle the sorts of problems we have been talking about (see Namboodiri, 1988). Its distinctive focus is organizations, which in the model are treated as components of larger social systems. Organizations are central, not incidental, to this model. The model can be described as follows:

Flows of activities are traced through in an interdependent system of organizations concerned with producing and distributing goods and services to consumer groups.

The model has the following characteristics:

- The central actors of this system are not individuals nor industries; they are formal organizations and networks of organizations, for example, which we regard as mechanisms for transforming a society's resources into products and services for its citizens.
- The flow of inputs and outputs is channeled and synchronized through diverse structures related to assorted outcomes.
- It is taken for granted that variable outputs can be explained by differences in structural forms, and, therefore, a central task of macrosociology is to account for this variance in structural form.

This model will be discussed in greater detail in the following chapters.

SUMMARY AND CONCLUSIONS

Macrosociology was defined as the systematic study of the unitary collective properties of organizations and organizational networks. That definition excludes microsociology, which we defined in the previous chapter as the study of selected attributes and behavior patterns of discrete members of a population of human beings. The striking thing about collectives is that they can be understood without reference to their individual members. We maintain that, since most of social life transpires in organizations, differences among organizations should account for outcomes at the macro level. Organizations should be sampled and used as the unit of analysis.

We, therefore, find it ironic that organizations have not been the primary focus in precisely the literatures where they are most salient. For example, organizations are seldom mentioned in studies of social structure as related to intermarriage; relationships between organizational capacity and conflict; and the world systems, modernization literature. The last area, though supposedly central to the idea of macrosociology, is laden with psychological bias and euphemisms about political consciousness, elite unity, and the like. These esoteric concerns obscure the fact that the major forces emanate from organizations.

We introduced another way to approach macrosociology. The input–output model traces flows of activities through an interdependent system of organizations concerned with producing goods and services and distributing them to consumer groups. We shall develop and illustrate this model throughout the remainder of this book. First, however, it will be worthwhile to review the alternatives. The following chapter is a commentary on several other models being used for macro-level analysis. Chapter 4 is devoted to one of them: network analysis. In the last part of the book, we will return to the input–output model for a more intensive look.

Chapter 3

Rival Paradigms of Organizations

We have been arguing that organizations should be the focus of macro-level research. If so, what is the best way to proceed? Which approaches are available, and can we improve on them? Among the possible options, we think three are worthy of serious consideration: contingency approaches, organizational ecology, and organization network models. They are the focus of this chapter.

THE CONTINGENCY APPROACH

The premise of this approach is that structures adapt to "fit" different contexts. For example, in an early study of three business organizations, Lawrence and Lorsch (1967) reached the conclusion that structural differentiation was directly related to the amount of change and diversification of their markets. To cope with change, they observed, an organization divides its tasks. Different parts take responsibility for a discrete aspect of the environment. Having become differentiated, it then must devote more effort to coordination, which requires centralized decision-making hierarchies. Note that the approach is primarily concerned with environmental constraints (which reduce options), not with the decision makers themselves.

Some other examples of this approach include:

- A study of the craft form of organization found that it was linked to the seasonal and made-to-order basis of construction work (Stinchcombe, 1959). The elements of craft organization include subcontracting, competitive bidding, and quality controls.
- Some research suggests that dynamic, decentralized organic structures form in turbulent, heterogeneous, and changing environments. Bureaucratic

structures evolve in stable, predictable environments (Burns and Stalker, 1961).

- A study of the methods organizations use to cope with natural disasters found a combined pattern of decentralization and centralization (Brouillette and Quarantelli, 1971). At each level of hierarchy, subunits assumed more autonomy; but within each unit, decisions became more centralized.

Types of Contingencies

Myriad contingencies significantly alter organizational structures and the outcomes. Two important ones are availability of resources and laws governing organizations.

Resource Dependence. The amount and availability of necessary resources is obviously critical. Every organization controls resources needed by others and, in turn, depends on them for what it does not have. Consequently, organizations are compelled to cooperate. Dependencies are especially pronounced among highly specialized organizations (Aiken and Hage, 1968; Cook and Emerson, 1984). Usually, when an organization possesses autonomy, prestige, and power, it can control more scarce resources (see Pfeffer, 1982).

Legislation and the Courts. Law exerts a powerful force on organizations, whether they are operating in the public sector or private sector (Bidwell and Kasarda, 1985; DiMaggio and Powell, 1983). Government regulation has kindled a new managerial revolution that, in effect, has transferred power from professional managers within a corporation to a vast cadre of government regulators (Weidenbaum, 1977).

Business organizations are protected and regulated through licenses, patents, copyrights, tariffs, and subsidies. There are laws governing consumer product safety, environmental pollution, equitable hiring practices, labor relations, and the like.

Public organizations, such as local school districts and state education agencies, are circumscribed in diverse ways, ranging from legislation and incorporation regulations to board policies, accreditation, and certification standards, budgeting cycles, and affirmative action quotas.

Examples of legislative impact abound:

- Equal Employment Opportunity Guidelines declare any selection procedure illegal if it adversely affects any race, sex, or ethnic groups (Danet, 1981).

- Unemployment compensation, compulsory union recognition, and protection for the collective bargaining process have reduced the economic dependency of workers on their employers and blunted managerial control in factories (Burawoy, 1983).

- White collar crimes invite further intervention from regulatory agencies (Braithwaite, 1985).

- Laws regulating patents and copyrights favor the pharmaceutical industry, giving it a higher margin of profit than the record industry (Hirsch, 1975).
- School districts have been unable to stop some popular but clearly inefficient programs, which are mandated by laws supported by powerful interests (Freeman, 1979).
- Government regulations affect organizational survival rates. For example, marginal businesses have been forced into bankruptcy by revised pollution laws requiring expensive equipment, and by tax codes undercutting advantages in depreciation schedules and capital gains taxes.
- The health care industry has been transformed by recent Medicare and Medicaid legislation, which adds the government as a third party to the doctor-patient relationship (Aldrich, 1979; Starr, 1982); the new system of payments for health care has provoked mergers, bankruptcies, and a proliferation of profit-making health organizations.

In all, contingency models call attention to interdependencies between organizational forms and specific conditions in the environment. There are three critical, but untested, assumptions that underlay contingency model:

1. There is an optimal fit between environments and structures.
2. This convergence occurs through structural adaptation.
3. Convergence enhances an organization's effectiveness and (implicitly) its survival chances.

ORGANIZATIONAL ECOLOGY

Organizational ecology treats organizations as members of distinctive populations, analogous to biological species competing for survival. This model is primarily concerned with (a) foundings, mergers, disbanding, and other vital events; and (b) how the presence and density of one population of organizations affects other populations (cf. Hannan and Freeman, 1989: 13–14). A special area, concerned with communities of organizations (called *fields*), is concerned with how links among populations affect the persistence of the community as a whole. Examples of organizational communities are populations of firms, populations of labor unions, and populations of regulatory agencies.

Advocates of organizational communities believe that organizational ecology is superior to contingency models. Carroll (1988: 1) has proclaimed, "Intellectually speaking, contingency theory is dead." However, in many respects, it is the same thing. Organizational ecology shares the first and third assumptions of the contingency framework. It differs only on how convergence occurs.

General Features

The parameters of the model can be grasped from a few underlying assumptions and some examples.

Assumptions. The most critical assumptions are:

- All organizations are in unrelenting competition with some others.
- Organizations are incapable of changing for many reasons. They include strong forces of inertia from sunken costs in buildings, equipment, and personnel; political resistance and legal restriction; reputation; and risks associated with change.
- Ultimately, organizations whose forms and practices, by chance, happen to be optimally suited for their situations are "selected out" to survive; unsuccessful forms disappear or are absorbed by other species.
- Organizations sharing the same environment will have similar forms; variance in forms increases with the number of environments (Hannan and Freeman, 1977; 1984; 1989).

A small group of researchers has been addressing assorted questions, such as:

- How does an environment with given characteristics shape the form of organizations in that environment?
- What are the chances that organizations having a given form will survive?
- What conditions promote new organizations?
- What accounts for the disappearance and emergence of entire *species* of organizations (e.g., why were blacksmiths replaced by auto mechanics)?

Examples. Organizational ecology is associated with research showing that

- new labor unions, electronics manufactures, and newspapers have higher death rates than older ones; unions are more likely than the others to disappear because of mergers (Freeman and Hannan, 1983).
- restaurants with general menus die off at rates different from ones with specialized menus. Their chances of survival depend on the frequency and extent of variation in sales (Hannan and Freeman, 1977).
- growth in wine imports stimulated the birth and expansion of domestic wineries seeking to participate in the expanding market (Delacroix and Solt, 1988: 53–70).
- there are positive correlations between the presence in a county of a local chapter of Mothers Against Drunken Driving and population size and growth, household income, education level, percentage of adults working in the county of residence, and the like (McCarthy, Wolfson, Baker, and Mosakowski, 1988).

- the rate at which growing school districts add and drop support staff differs from districts that are in a state of decline; supportive personnel hang on longer than teachers during downswings in enrollments (Freeman, 1979).

Is Organizational Ecology Useful?

Notwithstanding enthusiastic support from a circle of admirers, we do not find this model as useful as organizational network models, which will be considered next. We have several reservations, especially because it creates tough and unnecessary issues not associated with the other two models. The questions and reservations we raise below can help the reader weigh organizational ecology against the alternatives.

What Does the Model Contribute? Much of what poses as organizational ecology has been done before because most of the tenents are shared by other models. It has no monopoly, for instance, on the importance of the key variables, such as resource scarcity, environmental change and uncertainty, and other environmental contingencies. Hypotheses about age, size, liabilities of newness, and the administrative component come from other literatures, and, therefore, they can be tested without introducing premises from organizational ecology (Young, 1988).

At the same time, the most distinguishing (and controversial) feature of the model has not been an important theme in the ecology literature. Supposedly, organizations are incapable of adjusting; yet proponents of this presumption have not studied organizational change and innovation, which is understandable, because they do not believe in it. We acknowledge that the model has made some positive contributions. One is an insistent focus on mortality rates within samples of existing organizations. Another major advantage claimed for the model is that it can account for the emergence of new organizational forms. Yet most of the research so far has concentrated on new organizations arising within established populations, not the emergence of new population forms. It remains to be seen whether that topic can be more effectively addressed with this model than through historical research.

What Does the Nomenclature Add? Many terms have been invented, or borrowed from bioecology, to describe some common ideas. New organizations are *foundings*. If there is a demand for something, it is called a *niche*. An organization of a particular type is a *species*. Many organizations of the same type must be spoken of as a *population*. Congruence with some feature of an environment translates as "fit," and a good fit is nothing less than *isomorphism*. The crucial question is, what does the model say that is not already commonplace in the literature?

Why Not Adaptation? While inertia is an obstacle to planned change, organizations do change. They have adopted participatory management structures, equal opportunity hiring practices, decentralized forms of administration, franchising methods, and the like. They also have the power to alter their environments to improve the fit. For example, the automobile was an inefficient transportation method for densely populated cities, especially in a nation without good roads; yet the auto industry flourished. Why? Because it successfully lobbied congress and simultaneously converted miles of intraurban railways (which auto manufacturers purchased) into bus lines (Whitt, 1987). In much the same way, tobacco companies have survived hostile environments through lobbying and by developing international markets (Miles and Cameron, 1982).

Adaptation Is the Problem to Be Explained. To deny this capacity of organizations to change in response to threat, as Hannan and Freeman do, is unrealistic and misleading. It only diverts attention from the central issue, namely, to find out whether survival is more dependent on inertia than on capacity to change. It is a good bet that an organization can increase its life span if it chooses to make strategically selected changes. The dismissal of that possibility, while concentrating on survival rates, has led some investigators to take some positions for convenience, including these:

- Proposing to ignore the organizations that are trying to change.
- Redefining growth as the "death" of a small organization, followed by the "birth" of a big one.
- Ruling that mergers (and any other major transition state) should be treated as deaths (Hannan and Freeman, 1977).

Inertia Is Theoretically Trivial. A constant cannot account for variations in survival rates; hence, if all organizations are paralyzed by inertia, inertia cannot explain anything. This leaves us with chance. According to the doctrine of fate, whether one type of organization outlives another depends on luck, that is, the pure chance that its characteristics fit the environment better than characteristics associated with another type of organization.

However, the causes of so-called inertia are many and varied. Inertia appears to be a catchall term for all factors that impede or slow down change, including internal politics and external constraints. If so, focusing on those factors, individually or in groups, as other perspectives have done, is likely to provide more insight. Lumping them together in one broad, undifferentiated catagory is unproductive.

Death Is Only One of Many Important Transitions. The labels "inertia" and "change" are themselves misleading, since there is no clear line distinguishing something called *inertia* and something else called *change*. The reality is that a new organization will undergo many transitions before it dies. Depending on the observer's perspective, some of these transitions can be viewed either as expiration or as survival strategies that keep it alive in another form. Examples include diversification, reorganizations, mergers, and buyouts. When an organization goes through transitions like these, it usually brings about new relationships among partners within its network.

Therefore, we suggest, the important task is to find out whether all sorts of transitions can be predicted from the age structure and other properites of the organizations involved. Clearly, a narrow focus on mortality does not capture the full implications of the complex demographic issues that invite attention.

There Is a Continuum of Transitions. Instead of a dichotomy (i.e., life and death), change and mortality must be visualized as a *multistate transition problem.* Termination is only one of many transitions. This formulation avoids the thorny problem of establishing arbitrary dichotomies where something called *mortality* begins and something else called *survival,* or change, ends. It permits the investigator to recognize different kinds of changes and terminations. Attention can then be focused on explanatory models for transitions in this multistate space.

Competition: Is That All There Is? A meaningful population must have acquired, or be in the process of acquiring, unit character (Hawley, 1981: 120; Namboodiri, 1988: 622). However, in the organizational ecology literature, populations of organizations have been treated as aggregates with no known interrelationships to one another; none, that is, except a vague sense of ubiquitous "competition."

The presumption of ever-present competition nudges organizational ecology toward small, private-sector organizations, which often do see themselves in direct competition with one another. While small grocery stores in stable neighborhoods might meet this criterion, it does not apply to many others. In any case, competition is not a meaningful explanation of anything until pains are taken to measure the *amount* of competition involved.

From our reading of the situation, we conclude that two critical variables are being ignored: variation in the amount of competition, and noncompetitive relationships among organizations.

Variability in Risk from Competition. The degree of competition (sometimes even within the same population) will vary, for example, because some firms are favored by special subsidies or are riding the crest of rapid expansions of the market. Consequently, some markets will not be saturated with competitors, leaving room for nearly everyone. That could happen, for example, if demand for a new product outpaces supply (Astley, 1985).

Even under normal conditions, competition is not a big threat to everyone. For some of the most important producers, such as sprawling corporations and giant international franchises, survival depends less on competition than on having achieved favored political status via easy bank credit, favorable tax laws, bankruptcy safety nets, government bailouts, and advantageous trade barriers.

Noncompetitive Relationships. Besides competition, organizations also (a) cooperate in joint enterprises, (b) merge or form coalitions, (c) bargain and make exchanges, and (d) engage in open conflict. The courts, legislative bodies, and other third parties mediate conflict (Thompson and McEwen, 1958). There are many reasons that organizations might voluntarily enter into various kinds of cooperative relationships, including a need for one anothers' products and services, legal mandates to cooperate, common political and economic interests, and altruistic reasons.

Several patterns of twofold interactions have been documented in the literature. Each pattern describes how parties to a relationship affect each other (e.g., stimulate or suppress growth). If neither affects the other, the relationship may be called one of indifference. Other types of relationships include:

- *Full competition* – the presence of one organization suppresses the growth another;
- *Predatory competition* – one organization always gains at the expense of the other;
- *Bilateral reciprocity* – two organizations benefit from each others' presence;
- *Commensalism* – one organization benefits, while the other is unaffected (cf. Brittain and Wholey, 1988; Namboodiri, 1988: 630).

Note that these patterns refer to *outcomes* of dependencies as they affect the organizations involved. In Chapter 4, other concepts will be introduced that describe general *forms* of dependency (regardless of how their outcomes affect the organizations involved).

Any of these relationships can quickly change with shifting market conditions. Competition tends to vary inversely with demand. When the demand curve changes shape, the structure of competition can quickly change. For example, when consumer preferences switched from large cars to small ones, U.S. auto makers lost some of their competitive advantage to foreign companies accustomed to making fuel-efficient cars. Subsequently, American auto manufacturers formed partnerships with Japanese companies to produce small imports (cf. Zammuto and Cameron, 1985).

The population ecology model is not designed to address issues such as that because it treats organizations as aggregate units that function independently from one another. This assumption is required by some of the analytical techniques that are commonly employed in connection with this model. The validity (or lack of it) of assuming indepedence has not been given due attention in the literature.

Where Are the Population Boundaries? Research in this tradition has often failed to identify who the competitors are (Zucker, 1989). One study found that the effect of organizational density on mortality was less reliable in smaller geographical units than in large areas. This finding is hard to reconcile with reason, which suggests that there would be more competition in the smaller places. Density should have more impact on that population.

Zucker adds that density typically has been measured within one population (e.g., newspapers), yet we know that different populations compete with one another. Therefore, density should be measured more broadly. For example, television stations compete with newspapers for advertising customers. Neighborhood grocery stores face competition from many types of businesses besides similar stores in the immediate neighborhood. Their profit margins are affected by chain grocery stores throughout the metropolitan area, and by department stores, convenience stores, and even gas stations that sell groceries.

Types of Mortality. There are many forms of dependence besides competition; therefore, no one should be surprised to learn that competition is not the only thing that kills off organizations. Sometimes organizations are threatened for incidental reasons. Zammuto and Cameron (1985) point out that the market for fluorocarbon propellants collapsed after the government banned them. The legislation affected firms manufacturing and distributing the product even though it was not directed toward them.

Legal Causes of Mortality. Sometimes an organization will be directly attacked in legislation or lawsuits intended to put it out of business. For example, a local factory found guilty of repeatedly violating laws regulating public safety, health, and pollution may be ordered by the courts or licensing boards to cease operations.

Death by Decree. The Congress terminated the National Institute of Education (an agency of the Federal government) in still another way, namely, by *decree.* After a decade of repeated attacks by members of Congress and unsympathetic administrations, Congress decided not to fund it any longer. During the last decade, school boards have closed schools when enrollments dropped.

Death by Expiration. Many other organizations have been created for specified periods of time. They simply expire when they are supposed to. A federally funded experimental schools program, many job training demonstration programs, and aerospace manufacturers funded by the government have exited this way. Many of these decisions are based on political, educational, social need, and other criteria. Economic competition is not the only reason for mortality.

Death and Other Status Transitions. While it is sometimes easy to identify mortality, just as often death is indistinguishable from other status transitions. In which of the following cases shall we say the organization is gone?

- It begins to provide totally different products and services.
- It adopts a new name and moves to another country.
- It has new owners and managers.
- All of the personnel have been fired and replaced with different people.
- Many major policies are revised; a department store no longer gives credit and stops advertising in the local papers.
- It adopts different marketing strategies and establishes new subcontracting arrangements.

A company dropped off the *Fortune* list of the top 500 companies. Hannan and Freeman (1977) pronounced it dead. This is a baffling categorization. A restaurant changes its name and moves to another part of the city. Did it die? Suppose it also hires new waiters and cooks, and a different chef, and also switches menus from Chinese to Mexican food, but that it has the same owners, the same credit policies, and it is still about the same size. Is it dead or not?

The point we are making is that these are arbitrary classifications. They are neither constructive nor necessary. As applied to organizations, mortality is a variable. Often, there is no convenient, clear-cut point at which everyone will agree a social entity is dead. Mortality takes its place on a broad spectrum of status transitions, and therefore, it becomes secondary to other questions. Consider the following example:

A department store chain recently declared bankruptcy and was purchased by another chain. The name and ownership changed, as did some policies (e.g., credit cards were no longer accepted), and the quality of merchandise seemed to go down a notch. Most of the clerks and managers retained their jobs, though. From a customer's standpoint, there were few differences, except for some who were inconvenienced because a few stores were closed. Is this mortality? Why should anyone have to decide? What is important is that a transition state may or may not affect the output of goods and services.

Labeling a given transition state, or classifying organizations according to their various states of life and death, is not the most important task. What is important is to discover how any of the transitions affects the total output of a given set of organizations.

Does Organizational Mortality Make Any Difference? It is puzzling to find so much interest in why particular organizations do or do not survive, irrespective of the consequences for anything. Other status transitions can be more consequential for the society than the death of a few organizations. We see no reason to be preoccupied exclusively with deaths and foundings to the exclusion of administrative reorganization, fiscal restructuring, and expansion and contraction of product lines, or other changes that can affect the society at large.

Another Perspective

In contrast to conventional organizational ecology approaches, we take the position that

- what happens to the output of goods and services is more important than whether particular organizations survive.
- outcomes are the responsibility of a total set of interdependent organizations.
- in addition to competition, interdependence includes cooptation, coalition, bargaining, and conflict.

The unit of analysis, therefore, must be networks of interdependent organizations, not population aggregates consisting of unconnected units.

What Matters Is the Output. The question we regard as important is this: what happens to a total set of organizations after some of them die or change, and how do status transitions affect the outcomes? Consider subcontracting relationships. Suppose for a moment that three-fourths of the components of a certain "American" car come from ten companies scattered throughout the United States, Europe, and Japan. What will happen if some of the ten subcontractors go out of business? Maybe nothing. Whether mortality makes any difference will depend on how quickly existing or new companies step in to produce what is needed. Even if no one comes forward, the remaining companies could manage through growth and diversification, changing product lines, and the like.

Our point is that the mortality of ten organizations may or may not make any difference for the total output. What matters for the society depends on what happens to the total set of organizations. The functions of deceased organizations can be absorbed by existing or new ones. Hannan and Freeman (1977) never fully develop this point, although they recognize that a given level of demand can be met either by expanding existing organizations or by creating many smaller ones.

Therefore, the survival, or mortality, of particular organizations has no necessary relationship to the output and distribution of products and services within a society. The disappearance of some could reduce or improve the performance of the entire set. The survival of others could improve or reduce the output. There is no guarantee that the consequences will be any better because the survival rate is high.

Interdependency Is the Critical Issue. Organizational ecology treats populations of organizations as unbounded aggregates, connected only through hypothetical competition. Therefore, the model manages to mask entirely what, for us, is the central theoretical problem. The most important task, as we see it, is accounting for the conditions responsible for various forms of interdependency among organizations and the consequences.

Because many transition states affect the total output of goods and services, it does not make sense to focus on mortality and survival. Therefore, we are urging, research should focus on how age structure and the composition of organizational networks affect their total output of goods and services. This alternative will be introduced in the following paragraphs and developed further throughout the remainder of the book.

ORGANIZATIONAL NETWORK MODELS

If, as we contend, organizations are the primary actors in modern societies, it follows that the environment of any one organization consists of the actions of still others. In the words of one writer, organizations work together like a "froth of bubbles, constantly sharing or exchanging members, growing and dying, and being absorbed and segmented in response to changing conditions" (Pennings, 1981). They are mutually dependent, relying on one another to provide inputs (material and financial resources, legitimacy, members and clients) and to consume their products. Besides making exchanges, organizations often act in unison. By uniting, each organization can exercise more control, and possibly obtain more resources, than would be possible in isolation.

General Features

Organizational networks make up a distinct organizational form operating on their own logic and principles (cf. Powell, 1990). While they must operate within the boundaries of laws and customs, they are not constrained by an overriding administrative authority system as organizations are. They offer the advantages of institutional cooperation and exchange without totally compromising autonomy. The ability of organizations to make creative use of networks to their advantage can spell success or failure (Aldrich and Zimmer, 1986; Larson, 1991). Similarly, it has been suggested that the power and position of nations is determined by how they are related to powerful organizations.

Contrasts with Organizational Ecology. The contrast with organizational ecology is striking. As we observed, organizational ecology treats all organizations as competitors that otherwise have nothing to do with one another. Network approaches assume that all actors interact in social systems consisting of other actors capable of influencing one another (Knoke and Kuklinski, 1982: 9). Therefore, in addition to their intrinsic attributes, actors possess relational properties having both form and content.

Organizational ecology does not address the types of issues that network models handle best. However, network models can address issues that conventionally have been associated with organizational ecology. For example, the chances that a given set of organizations will survive depends upon whether they have dependable suppliers and customers, are able to obtain favorable loans, and can count on powerful sponsors. In other words, survival rates hinge on the pattern of connections among organizations.

Types of Relationships within Networks. The kind of relational forms characteristic of networks include how frequently organizations interact (intensity), how much they affect each other (influence), and how often they engage in joint activities (partnership) (see also Knoke and Kuklinski, 1982: 15). Some common types of network relationships are:

- *Transactions* (i.e, exchanges of goods and services)
- *Instrumental relations* (i.e., contacts for valuable goods, services or information)
- *Communication* (i.e., informing another organization about the consequences of using its products)
- *Boundary penetration* (i.e., overlapping memberships; e.g., an officer of one organization is on another's board of directors)
- *Authority/power relations* (i.e., member organizations authorize a coordinating body to speak for them; e.g., the National Council of Churches)
- *Kinship* (i.e., bonds among family members, which can entail any of the above types of relationships)
- *Sentiment relations* (i.e., expressions of affection, admiration, deference, and hostility), especially among dyads (Knoke and Kuklinski, 1982: 15–16).

Assumptions of the Basic Model. The basic model rests on the following assumptions:

- The environment that is most pertinent for any organization is other organizations (Aldrich, 1979).
- Organizations form interdependent networks connected through utilitarian exchanges, through legal and political coercion, and through normative example and pressures.

- Network partners need not be aware of one another, since they may be indirectly connected through third parties; indirect relationships are based on more complex and abstract expectations than are direct relationships (Kadushin, 1981).
- Patterns of interdependency are influenced and buffered by their internal structures.

The above four assumptions define the basic model. We shall extend it by adding two more:

- The output and distribution of products and services in a society is dependent upon patterns of relationships within and among networks of organizations.
- Within limits, a given level of goods and services can be achieved from different mixes of various kinds of organizations, and, alternatively, organizations can change their forms and activities to maintain or increase this level of goods and services.

Networks as Input–Output Transactions

These two assumptions go beyond the network models being used at the present time. We have borrowed them from the input–output framework mentioned earlier because they add extraordinary power to the conventional model. We propose to treat an entire network as a production system having some kind of output(s).

Many people make assumptions about linkages between structure and outcomes. For example, government agencies often rotate research grants among states, universities, and research centers. It is assumed either that it makes no difference which particular organizational units are involved (in which case, outcomes will remain constant) or that it does make a difference (and, hence, outcomes will thereby change). In either case, the policy maker is making implicit assumptions about linkages between structural components and outcomes. The input–output approach keeps the focus steadfastly on goods and services produced. It requires a researcher to account for variability in outcomes via both patterns of relationships within and between networks and characteristics of the member organizations.

An Illustration. A few implications of the model can be illustrated with schools. They have become formally and informally specialized in response to a wide range of demands. Some stress vocational education, or college preparation. Others emphasize driver's training, information about health and sex, citizenship, sports, and the like. Some skills, such as drivers' education, are uniformly in demand across all segments of society. The demand for other skills, such as mathematics, is variable and uneven.

In this context, a national debate has erupted over whether some schools are superior to others. Some research suggests that private schools produce better academic and moral outcomes. The academic goal has been the focus of much of the controversy (Coleman and Hoffer, 1987). However, public schools may be better at vocational education, processing large numbers of students, assimilating individuals from diverse cultural backgrounds, managing different types of behavioral and learning difficulties, or the like. We conclude, therefore, that the ability of a community to meet these various demands requires the contributions of both public and private schools. In other words, the mix of forms, and interdependencies between them, may be more critical than whether one or the other produces better academic results.

This point has been overlooked in the national debate on this issue. It is fruitless to go on trying to establish the superiority of one type of school over another. Instead, we should find out how a given mix of private and public schools affects each outcome being asked of schools. Solutions will hinge on finding an optimal mix among not only these two types of schools but other forms of education as well (e.g., trade schools).

Implications

Four implications of consequence follow when the focus is changed from organizational units to the goods and services produced by networks of organizations acting in concert. They are:

1. Outcomes are determined by the composition of the set.
2. Mortality is only one form of status transition.
3. Network boundaries follow dependencies.
4. What matters is the distribution of outcomes.

Each will now be discussed.

Outcomes Are Determined by Composition of the Set. First, under the principle of substitution, there is no one-to-one correspondence between organizational structures and outputs. For example, Chinese food can be served by home delivery or carry-out stores, specialized or general menu restaurants, street carts, stalls in shopping malls, frozen food, or delicatessen departments in grocery stores, and homes. It follows that the composition of a set of organizations can change without affecting the output.

- New organizations develop to make up for those that have died.
- The outputs of failed organizations are provided by survivors.
- Survivors adopt characteristics of those they have displaced.

For example, it is plausible that as the percentage of private schools increases, they will begin to assume some of the characteristics and functions of public schools. Another example: large department stores now sell many of the products at one time distributed by small dime stores.

One may lament the demise of dime stores, but from our perspective, the fundamental questions concern whether changes have occurred in goods and services as the distribution of large and small retail outlets has changed. For example, has the availability, range, price, and composition of the goods distributed changed? Have the labor force characteristics changed?

A consumer does not necessarily care whether one type of restaurant has a better or worse chance of surviving than others. What is of greater significance for the consumer, as well as for the community and the society, is whether the kinds of meals people want stay available after their favorite restaurants have expired. If there are more restaurants than needed, the demise of some is not significant in the total picture. For example, if all Chinese restaurants were to go out of existence, it would make no difference to society, provided that (a) general menu restaurants began to serve authentic Chinese food; or (b) dual forms of restaurants evolve, which are capable of serving both general and specialized menus under one roof.

Mortality Is Only One Form of Status Transition. The second implication is that organizational mortality is only one of a variety of status transitions affecting output, and it is often *less* important than others. For example, organizations increase and decrease in prestige, power, wealth, size, technical competence, and other dimensions of status. They also change forms, from partnerships to corporations, through mergers, buyouts, reorganizations, and franchising. It is likely that the consequences for customers, tax collection agencies, employees, and other sectors will be more significant than survival rates.

If the focus is kept steadfastly on the output of the total set of organizations, the task is to observe what the consequences of the change have been. Establishing firm criteria for pronouncing death becomes trivial. For example, when two organizations merge, what matters is what happens to the network of organizations and its clients. Which one has survived is immaterial.

When one organization buys out another, perhaps something, from a legal standpoint, has died. Or shall we say something was born? It does not really matter. If the entity continues to operate as before, and if it provides the same services, then for the tax agencies and customers at least, little of consequence has happened. It has merely transformed status. If some employees are fired, the consequences depend on how the action affects relationships with other organizations—unions, law firms, placement agencies, competitors who have new access to skills and inside knowledge, government oversight agencies concerned with unemployment compensation or fair practices, and the like.

Network Boundaries Follow Dependencies. The third implication that follows from shifting the focus away from specific organizations to outputs is that it redefines the relevant populations of interest. Consider restaurants. From a population perspective, they would be the focus; restaurants compete with one another. But, from a network perspective, restaurants are part of an organized food production and distribution industry. This industry includes many otherwise obscure organizational units that also provide meals. Among them are families; street vendors; dormitories; airlines; vending machine companies; social clubs; churches; and cafeterias sponsored by schools, government agencies, and businesses. Placing restaurants within such a network, then, changes the spheres of dependency. In some sense, all of these places compete with one another. However, since they provide different products and services, they may all gain (bilateral reciprocity), or most of them may be unaffected by the presence of the others (commensalism).

In their study of restaurants, Hannan and Freeman (1977; 1989) were concerned with the failure rates of two types of establishments: general menu restaurants and specialized restaurants. They assume these two types of eating places are competing primarily with each other. When the environment is in a state of rapid transition, they find that general menu establishments have higher survival rates than those with specialized menus. But, how can we know from where the fiercest competition is coming? It could come from other kinds of places that serve food. We do not know that general menu restaurants survive at the expense of special menu establishments, or the reverse. Indeed, the supply of potential customers for conventional restaurants appears to be very elastic. Both general and special menu restaurants can flourish to the extent they are successful in competing with other sources of prepared foods.

What Matters Is the Distribution of Outcomes. Here, we are repeating ourselves. However, it is worth emphasizing again that the model we are advocating is ultimately concerned with comparative rates of change in different distributions over time. For example, the distribution of schools practicing tracking has changed shape during the past twenty years. Has there been a corresponding change in the distribution of job placements? Another example: Schools in the upper end of the tracking distribution may differ in their division of labor, special facilities, staffing patterns (e.g., specialists, teacher/pupil ratio), proportion of students promoted out of lower tracks, time spent in school, school district resources, and the like. Any of these properties could either offset or transform otherwise detrimental effects of tracking.

Since different properties (or combinations thereof) can potentially produce the same result, it is unrealistic to focus on only one characteristic at a time.

Because the effects of a given structure can be modified in the presence of others, it is necessary to construct measures of structural configuration. Distributions of this measure can then be correlated with outcome distributions along with each structural characteristic considered separately.

SUMMARY AND CONCLUSIONS

Having concluded that organizations are the proper focus of macro-level research, we considered in this chapter the appropriate model to use. Three options were deliberated: contingency models, organizational ecology models, and organization network models.

Contingency Models

We saw that *contingency models* call attention to interdependencies between organizational forms and specific conditions in the environment. They assume that (1) there is an optimal fit between environments and organizational structures, (2) convergence occurs through adaptation, and (3) convergence enhances an organization's effectiveness and (implicitly) its survival chances.

Organizational Ecology

Organizational ecology shares the first and third assumptions, differing only on how convergence occurs. The ecology approach postulates natural selection rather than structural adaptation. We questioned this model's assumptions, especially that organizations can function autonomously, are always in a state of fierce competition, and cannot change. We also questioned the overemphasis on organizational mortality and challenged its significance.

Macrosociology, we concluded, is better served by organizational network models than by organizational ecology models. The latter tend to totally ignore the relational context, transitions other than births and deaths, and the capacity of organizations to form networks so as to influence their own destiny.

Organizational Network Models

Unlike organizational ecology, *network approaches* assume that all actors participate in social systems consisting of other actors capable of influencing one another. Therefore, in addition to their intrinsic attributes, organizations possess relational properties having both form and content. Relational forms include the frequency of the relationship (intensity) and level of joint involvement in the same activities.

An Input–Output Model. None of these models incorporates what we regard as the critical significance of organizations, namely, producing and distributing goods and services for a society. We have argued that

- what happens to the output of goods and services is more important than whether particular organizations survive;
- outcomes are the responsibility of a total set of interdependent, but interchangeable, organizations; and
- cooptation, coalition, bargaining, and conflict are as important as competition.

The appropriate unit of analysis is networks of interdependent organizations, not population aggregates consisting of unconnected units. Therefore, the researcher must consider, what happens to the total set of organizations after some of them expire or change and how do these and other transitions affect the outcomes? The input–output model that was proposed is based on the following premises:

- There is no one-to-one correspondence between organizational structures and outputs.
- The composition of a set of organizations can change without affecting the output.
- Organizational mortality is only one of a variety of status transitions that affects output, and it is often less important than others.
- The way relevant populations of interest are defined must be reconsidered.

Implications

The approach we are advocating is not novel. It is widely used in practice and in theory. The linkage between structure and outcomes is a central task of structural functionalism, systems theory, and other paradigms. Accordingly, linkages between structures and outcomes have been debated for many years by organizational theorists. That is our point. We believe that organizational network models will serve macrosociology better than will organizational ecology. There is no better way to understand macro phenomena than to focus on the output and distribution of goods and services in a society. Therefore, the remainder of this book is exclusively concerned with this topic. The network approach, which was briefly introduced in this chapter, will be developed throughout the remainder of this book.

CHAPTER 4

Organizational Networks

The previous chapter introduced organizational networks. A *network of organizations* is a specific social structure consisting of all connected relationships among affiliated collectivities (Aldrich, 1979: 387). This notion evolved from the sociometric analysis. The latter is concerned with identifying friendship circles, work groups, and other types of social ties among individuals.

Networks function as political economies. A *political economy* is made up of powerful, interdependent actors, whose purpose is to control scarce resources, such as money, raw materials, personnel, customers, and legitimacy. Dependency increases inversely with the number of providers and outlets for products and services (Evan, 1972). An organization gains power over others by getting control of resources they need. Power, in turn, enables it to obtain still more resources (Benson, 1975; Zald, 1970).

Laumann and Knoke (1987) describe "the modern industrial polity" as a complex of formal organizations in conflict with one another over the collective allocation of scarce societal resources. This view is consistent with the political economy framework, except that organizations do not always engage in conflict. To increase their collective leverage over other coalitions, groups of organizations unite, exchange goods and services, and work out mutually beneficial bargains and goals.

REASONS FOR INTERORGANIZATIONAL NETWORKS

Organizations form relationships for countless reasons, which include obtaining or sharing resources, exercising power, coordinating joint ventures, and complying with laws and administrative requirements.

Incentives

For convenience, those reasons can be reduced to three types of incentives: coercive, normative, and utilitarian (see Hall and associates, 1977).

Coercive Incentives. Often, organizations have no choice but to cooperate to meet legal and social obligations. For example, U.S. manpower training legislation requires local employment services to work with public aide offices.

Normative Incentives. On the other hand, they frequently cooperate to promote common interests through joint ventures. One example is collaboration among units of local police and fire departments and the national guard during riots and natural disasters. Local businesses often unite to oppose taxes or proposed legislation, or to support a school bond levy.

Utilitarian Incentives. Other reasons for collaboration include: (a) obtaining information and financial and human resources, and (b) cultivating outlets for products and services (Aiken and Hage, 1968; Cook and Emerson, 1984; Laumann and Knoke, 1987: 13).

Advantages and Consequences of Networks

These three incentives, in combination, render compelling forces to form networks. However, from a different perspective, we may say networks yield fundamental benefits for the society as a whole, not just for the organizations involved. Two consequences that are particularly critical are coordinating individual efforts and channeling power.

Coordination. One advantage of collaboration is to coordinate the joint efforts and activities among discrete organizations. For example, a training center agrees to supply a client organization with a fixed number of workers during the year. The arrangement stabilizes demand for its services, enabling it to realistically set limits on admissions. When an organization specializes narrowly but shares responsibility for overlapping functions with other organizations, it can be more effective if it works with them. Each organization can restrict its attention to a specific aspect of a large problem while benefitting from the results of the total effort.

While coordination can be achieved in many ways, two are of special importance: interlocking directorate structure and coalitions.

Interlocking Directorates. The largest American corporations, especially those in the most concentrated industries, are governed by interlocking boards whose members sit on more than one such board (Pennings, 1980). Members obtain and share information and ideas. Financial institutions and industrial firms have dominated the boards of U.S. firms since 1935. They are segmented into distinct and densely connected cliques representing specific geographical or financial interest groups (Mizruchi, 1982).

Coalitions. Besides being linked through board memberships, organizations enter directly into coalitions. For example, independent universities within a state form federations whose purpose is to share research facilities and information about opportunities for research and to work out a domain of consensus so they will not be competing against one another for major grants.

Power. Organizations also can enhance their power through their memberships and affiliations with powerful organizations. Selznick's (1949) path breaking study of the Tennessee Valley Authority (TVA) described a coalition between farmers and college professors who formed a political lobby whose goal was to oppose another federal agency. Useem (1984) maintains that an inner circle of corporate executives, whose purpose is to protect their common corporate interests, has formed in the United States; however, Useem has been challenged (see, for example, Burt, 1983a; 1983b; Ornstein, 1984). Studies have shown that

- women's professional groups and neighborhood development agencies have better chances of surviving when they are supported by established professional groups or influential politicians than when unsupported (Wiewel and Hunter, 1985).

- organizations with formal ties to financial institutions can achieve larger budgetary increases and profits (Burt, 1983a; Pennings, 1980).

- community agencies that are closely associated with elites have more success than the others in obtaining budget requests from the local United Way organizations; this advantage is even stronger if they also operate expensive programs jointly with other agencies (cited in Pfeffer, 1982; see also Pfeffer and Salancik, 1978).

- leadership within communities is exercised by a small, easily identified, group of persons who simultaneously hold high-level policy positions within not one, but many organizations (Perrucci and Pilisuk, 1970).

TYPES OF NETWORKS

Four basic types of networks can be identified using two distinctions. First, lateral networks can be distinguished from organizational sets. Second, both can be studied from either a focal perspective or from a global one.

Networks and Sets Distinguished

Two general patterns formed by collectivities are lateral networks and organizational sets (Caplow, 1964; Aldrich and Whetten, 1981).

Lateral Networks. A *lateral network* consists of autonomous organizations, each of which performs a different function within a division of labor. An example is a high school, the families associated with it, taxpayer groups interested in school levies, businesses that hire students and graduates, colleges attended by graduates, and accrediting agencies.

Many types of relationships can form among the organizations participating in lateral networks. They do not necessarily compete directly with one another, although they may compete. Sometimes they depend on one another's goods and services. For example, high schools depend on colleges to supply teaching personnel. In other cases, they satisfy a different need for distinct segments of the market and, therefore, do not compete, although they may provide roughly the same type of goods and services. For example, a school cafeteria provides noonday meals to third grade children, while a four-star exclusive restaurant serves meals to elite diners during the late evening hours. While they are engaged in the same business, they are not competing for customers.

Network relationships are complex, and, therefore, the same organizations cooperate and compete at different times, and with respect to different functions. For example, the high schools and colleges in the above illustration might be in contention for limited tax dollars, and cafeterias and restaurants might vie for managers and food handlers.

Relationships among the organizations in a lateral network can be indirect as well as direct. Suppose, for example, that a city tax office rules that a company is no longer entitled to deduct, from taxes owed, the cost of a product it usually buys from another firm. Suppose, too, that the ruling prompts it to stop buying the product from the supplier. Then we may say the tax office is an indirect participant in this buyer–seller relationship.

Organizational Sets. An *organizational set* is composed of competitive organizations that do the same thing and share a common resource base and normative system (Caplow, 1964). Examples include elementary schools within a school district, baseball teams in the American League, and hospitals belonging to a local hospital federation.

There are practical differences between the two forms. An organizational set, like a baseball team, competes for the same players and fans. However, members of the set agree to abide by common norms regarding acceptable conduct, standards of competence, recruiting rules, and geographical domains. Also, they share a common prestige system. These norms regulate the competition and establish acceptable and unacceptable conduct. Often, organizations create their own associations to help assure that the rules will be enforced.

In contrast, members of lateral networks usually do not compete so directly, and they typically do not subscribe to a unique rule system. For example, insurance companies, hospitals, and funeral homes do

Figure 4.1
A Hypothetical Focal Network

A hypothetical organization, "*Community Hospital*," can be used to illustrate an exchange system comprised of input and output organizations mediated by regulatory and throughput organizations concerned with how the organization functions.

A Hypothetical Illustration

Input Organizations:

▸ Sources of Patients: Clinics, doctors' offices, emergency services.

▸ Sources of Personnel: Medical schools, nursing schools, employment agencies.

▸ Sources of Supplies: Pharmaceutical companies, food distributors, medical supply
   companies.

▸ Sources of Income: Insurance companies, social welfare agencies.

Throughput (Service) Organizations:

▸ Ambulance services, accounting firms, janitorial services, phone companies, laundries.

Regulatory Organizations:

▸ The American Medical Association, nursing organizations, fire marshals, food
   inspectors, insurance companies, government agencies.

Output Organizations:

▸ Funeral homes, nursing homes, medical clinics, psychiatric agencies, trash collection
   services.

not compete simultaneously for the same clients; they do not subscribe to the same rule system; and they do not belong to the same professional associations.

Focal and Global Perspectives Distinguished

Interorganizational networks can be analyzed from either a focal perspective or a global perspective. In addition, there is a modified focal perspective, referred to here as the "extended focal perspective." We will next describe these different patterns.

The Focal Perspective. The *focal perspective* concentrates on a particular organization within a network of organizations that supplies its inputs and uses its outputs. All relations in the network are linked back to this (focal) organization (Evan, 1972). For example, a hospital does business with dozens of insurance companies, hires nurses from many hospital training programs, and works with many funeral homes and nursing homes. A more detailed illustration is provided in Figure 4.1. The simple inventory in the figure is compounded in reality by differences in the practices used by role partners. For example, a hospital doing business with dozens of insurance companies must cope with different forms, deadlines, and eligibility criteria. Complications often arise when there are many sets of rules, which produces pressures to standardize practices.

The investigator can measure the general pattern in a variety of ways. As one index of specialization, one might use the ratio of organizations that supply inputs in relation to the number of organizations that receive outputs. An index of dependency, and hence the potential of a given organization dominating the relationship, is the number of suppliers of a given commodity. However, these are simple measures. There is a better way to measure dominance.

Measuring Dominance. The power of a focal organization is a function of its dependency relationships within a network of suppliers and buyers. One measure of a group's positional power is the number of first-tier suppliers who purchase its output directly plus a second-tier group who, in turn, buys from the direct purchasers (Perrone, 1984). One can tabulate a hierarchy of economic dominance based on each group's ability to disrupt the economy by suspending their productive activity. It is obtained by taking into account both direct and indirect purchasers (Perrone, 1984). Following is an example of positional power:

If Industry 1 provides outputs to Industries 2 and 3 but is not dependent on their outputs, a strike in Industry 1 will have greater disruptive potential than if it were to occur in the other two industries. Since workers providing essential services potentially can be very disruptive, they often can obtain their demands without actually resorting to a work stoppage.

Actors who are not directly involved in the economic exchanges must be included when they have a vital interest in the outcomes. This includes the courts, government bodies, sympathetic unions, and private citizens (Wright, 1984). Such groups can exert enough coercive or normative power to tip the balance of economic power.

The Extended Focal Perspective. The focal perspective can be extended by making a cluster of organizations the focus instead of concentrating on only one organization. A cluster could include

- a mix of organizations with overlapping products, such as big department stores, shoe stores, and clothing shops within a state.
- an organizational set of interacting organizations, all of which have the same type of output. For example, one might use all hospitals in a city as the focus, and then examine the interdependencies of this set of organizations with suppliers, regulatory agencies, and organizations like nursing homes that use their output.

The Global Perspective. Even in extended form, the focal perspective distorts the importance of a few organizations. Consequently, it is incapable of addressing the most fundamental property of networks: *distribution patterns* among members of a network. The focus dwells on characteristics of specific organizations and not on how resources, influence, and power are distributed through structural relationships. Perhaps such a myopic view can be justified when only a few actors are dominant. However, more typically, different actors dominate different types of relationships in various circumstances.

The *global perspective* does not have this disadvantage. It is concerned with aggregate patterns in the network as a whole. For example, in some networks a few organizations, which control resources and make decisions for the entire network, dominate their partners. This is one type of aggregate pattern. In others, all organizations have an equal voice. This is another aggregate pattern. This approach assumes that

- power and resources are properties of the system as a whole, instead of something possessed by individual members.
- network outcomes are products of general patterns, such as the distribution of power and division of labor among network members.

These patterns can make a real difference in the outcomes. For example, research could be designed to find out whether networks with centralized coordinating bodies produce different types and amounts of goods and services than decentralized ones.

PROPERTIES OF NETWORKS

The global perspective will be used in the remainder of this discussion. Using this perspective, the observer can describe network patterns by finding the ties between all organizations in a population (Aldrich, 1979: 281). The ties identified can be used to describe different forms of dependence, network structures, and linking mechanisms.

Forms of Dependence

Dependency can take any of three general forms, namely, the *symbiotic form*, the *coalition form*, and the *adversary form*. In symbiotic relationships, the output of one organization is an input to the other. For example, since high school graduates attend college, we may say that high schools and colleges have a symbiotic relationship. Coalition-type relationships refer to voluntary cooperation and joint programs among autonomous organizations (Warren, 1967; Aldrich, 1979: 387). High schools often form partnerships with local businesses to provide work-study students with part-time employment and apprenticeships. Adversary-type relationships can take either of two forms:

1. *Competition* occurs when a fixed quantity of resources is controlled by third parties who are responsible for distributing them between two or more organizations.
2. *Conflict* occurs when some organizations directly block the others' access to resources (Schmidt and Kochan, 1972).

Differences between Competition and Conflict. The difference between competition and conflict can be illustrated as follows. Third parties regulate competition. Conflict involves direct confrontation between the parties involved. For example, fire and police departments compete for funds from a fixed tax base. The two departments usually do not directly confront each other. Their fates depend on decisions made by city councils, voters, and other third parties. Therefore, the key relationships are focused on third parties, not each other. However, if the police and fire units organize public protests complaining about one another and form picket lines to disrupt each other's work, they are in conflict.

Hypotheses. While pondering differences between various types of relationships, we raised some questions, either implicitly or explicitly, that now can be stated as hypotheses. For example, we hypothesize that the probability that relationships will become adversarial

- increases with the degree of overlap in the organization's outputs and scarcity of resources (cf. White, 1961).
- declines with demand (cf. Warren, Rose, and Bergunder, 1974).
- declines with volatility.[1]
- declines as some organizations become more dependent than others, thus increasing stability.

Forms of Dependency Compared to Outcomes. We have just defined three forms of dependence—symbiotic, coalition, and adversary. In Chapter 3, we defined four different terms pertaining to the effects of a dependence relationship—*bilateral reciprocity, commensalism, full competition,* and *predatory competition.* Recall that

- in bilateral reciprocity, two organizations benefit from the presence of each other.
- commensalism means that one organization benefits, while the other is unaffected.

- under full competition, the presence of one organization suppresses the growth of another.
- when the competition is predatory, one organization always gains at the expense of the other.

Note that these terms describe relationships that have *effects* on the participants, whereas we have just introduced other terms referring to *forms* of dependence.

Now, we may ask, how are the two sets of terms related? There are some obvious points of overlap. For example, full and predatory competition are outcomes of adversarial relationships. Also, perhaps one can assume that coalition relationships will last longer if two organizations benefit bilaterally. Nevertheless, the two sets are not identical. The research challenge is to determine the empirical relationships between form and outcome.

Envision, then, a two-way table using the four forms we described above as the rows, namely, symbiotic, coalition, and adversarial competition and conflict. The columns consist of the four outcomes, namely, bilateral reciprocity, commensalism, full competition, and predatory competition. We would want to know differences in the joint occurrences (i.e., cell frequencies). We also would want to investigate conditions that can account for differences in these frequencies.

Network Structures

Like an organization, a network has a formal authority structure, informal status system, and a division of labor. In addition, networks can be distinguished by their geographical properties.

Authority Structures. Some networks take the form of decentralized federations. Others function as centralized, corporate bodies (Warren, 1967). A *federation* is governed by a coordinating body, which is controlled by the members. Its responsibilities are limited to coordinating activities and promoting communication among the membership. For example, the National Chamber of Commerce represents locals in ways they agree to, but it cannot set policy for them.

In networks that have *corporate-type structures,* on the other hand, central bodies have authority to control the members. An example is an allied supreme military command headquarters for a multinational war effort, which is responsible for making the decision to invade a hostile nation. Another example is the Vatican dictating many aspects of Catholic churches throughout the world.

Levine and White (1961) compared corporate-type medical care networks with more decentralized, federated types. They found that the corporate networks depended less on the local health care system for resources, and, consequently, members of centralized networks interacted less with the local health care providers.

Informal Status Hierarchies. Besides formal arrangements, status hierarchies evolve from differences in prestige and access to resources (Klatzky, 1970). For example, the career mobility of school superintendents is tied to school district size.

Specialization. Another structural dimension is the amount of specialization within the hierarchy. Organizations formally and informally divide mutual responsibilities among themselves. For example, a network consisting of a dozen publicly funded research and development organizations divided responsibilities as follows: one served as coordinator of information and meeting agendas, another handled political pressures, another focused on developing vocational education curricula, and another took responsibility for distributing new curricular materials.

Relationships among specialized sets of organizations can affect the output of the network. Two examples follow:

1. An institution such as "public education" is in reality a network of accrediting agencies, testing organizations, textbook publishers, government bureaus, teacher training institutions, schools, colleges, and professional organizations. The relationships among these components can affect stability and change in the member organizations. For example, Wayland (1963) described barriers to curriculum change arising because of the time and effort it takes to incorporate new information into standardized tests, to certify the teachers, and to accredit agencies to endorse the new setup.
2. Clark (1965) described a different group of organizations that fostered curriculum change. Composed of government and private agencies, universities, and textbook publishers, this coalition introduced modern mathematics into most schools within record time. The "new math" swept into schools across the nation in record time through concerted action by federal funding agencies, teacher workshop programs, teacher training institutions, and committees of college professors.

Geographical Concentration. Geography sets parameters that force networks to behave in characteristic ways. Some networks consist only of organizations doing business within a given community; others include national headquarters, or international offices, associated with satellites scattered beyond the community.

Types of Networks Based on Geographical Concentration. Using these patterns, it becomes possible to classify networks based on percentage of member organizations that are

1. Associated with more than one geographical location *(dispersion);*

2. Locally owned or controlled (versus those controlled by absentee owners) *(localism);*
3. With primarily local (versus national or international) markets *(scope).*

Industrial and Commercial Cities. Two extremes, or *ideal-type* cities, might be delineated as follows:

- The *industrial city* emphasizes wholesale trade. It has national markets for its products; plants are strategically placed around the country or world base on economic considerations, such as available labor supply. It is absentee-owned and controlled from headquarters located in Atlanta, Detroit, or New York. Consequently, its leaders do not become involved in local projects or issues unless they are directly affected.
- The *commercial city* specializes in hotels, department stores, and professional and other retail services geared to local markets. It is owned and managed by local merchants, and the need for customers gives it an incentive to attract trade from the immediate area. Consequently, it supports taxes and provides some labor needed for civic, recreational, and cultural activities that will attract customers to the area.

Linking Mechanisms. Organizations can be directly linked in at least three ways:

- *Interpenetrations* of organizations through overlapping memberships; examples are parent–teacher associations, or members of a civic club who serve on a fund-raising drive for an art gallery.
- Interactions at the boundaries via specialists in fulfilling *boundary roles* (e.g., a school truant officer who works with members of the local police department).
- Interaction through *coordinating agencies* such as consortiums (Laumann and Knoke, 1987: 13), for example, member colleges participating in an intercollegiate athletic association (Guetzkow, 1966).

In the order listed, the linkages decrease in the diffuseness of influence that one organization can exercise over another. In the first type, outsiders' influence will not be limited to specific areas and thus can be felt in a variety of unspecified ways. In the third type, the influence will be highly circumscribed.

Boundaries. The boundaries of a network can be identified from two dimensions: (a) the frequency that a group of organizations directly or indirectly *interact* with one another, and (b) whether they *influence* each other directly or indirectly (cf. Corwin and Wagenaar, 1976). Organizations that do not interact or influence each other can be treated as being outside the network. However, since both interaction and influence are variables, the investigator needs to establish some cutting points based on the circumstances and problem being investigated.

Boundary Profiles. Combining interaction and influence makes it possible to derive *boundary profiles.* If we divide both variables into dichotomies, there are four boundary profiles:

- *High interaction/low influence.* Members of this type of network interact frequently but do not control one another. Organizations that do not interact on a frequent basis are not counted as members; thus there are no cases of dominant organizations.
- *Low interaction/high influence.* The members do not interact much, but when they do, some of them influence or control the others; or they all exercise some influence by making bargains and trade-offs.
- *High interaction/high influence.* This pattern describes a cohesive network.
- *Low interaction/low influence.* This pattern is characteristic of a loose-knit federation in which all members retain a high degree of autonomy and social distance. For example, members meet only when there is a crisis and act only if there is full consensus.

SOURCES OF NETWORK PATTERNS

There are manifold conditions shaping and altering network structures. This section mentions a few, such as goals and commitments of the member organizations, how they are set up and operate, and technologies they use; amount of turbulence in the environment; size of the network, its domain, and consensus on domain boundaries; degree of interdependence and competition within the network; and structure of the community, region, or nation.

Conditions within Organizations

The way a cluster of organizations relate to each other is affected by conditions within each of the organizations involved. In this regard, one study found the likelihood of organizations cooperating in joint programs increases directly with their complexity, number of new programs in which they are involved, and amount of communication going on within them (Aiken and Hage, 1968). The opportunities for members to participate in decisions and the number of rules and other measures of formalization had little effect (Hage, 1980). Other conditions that conceivably affect external relations include the organization's goals and other commitments it makes, how boundary roles are set up, and the type of technology the organization uses.

Goals and Commitments. Levine and White (1961) found that relationships among hospitals depended on their goals and other commitments. The most obvious example of this proposition is when hospitals have similar goals. They will find themselves competing for the same patients, which will affect their other relationships. In addition, goals and commitments can operate more subtly by altering an organization's structure, which, in turn, can alter relationships with outsiders. For instance, hospitals that had made a commitment to treat indigent, low-income minorities operated large outpatient clinics. These clinics attracted low-income, indigent patients, who then brought the hospital into contact with social agencies, the police, and federal welfare programs.

Boundary Structure. Internal structures that affect relationships with other organizations in a network include

- proportion of members involved in boundary relationships.
- degree to which boundary relationships are specialized within a few roles or departments.
- number of organizations involved.

We expect that the output of an organization will vary with the following:

- Number of boundary personnel, their status within their respective organizations, and relative to one another;
- Amount of time and other resources devoted to boundary relationships;
- Number of clients and customers, the volume of sales and services, and the number of contacts made; and
- Whether contacts are made in person, by phone, or by mail.

When a different specialist each works with different organizations, conflicts may develop among specialists as they cope with constituencies having diverse needs and making inconsistent demands on them. For example, in a hospital, one person handles medical insurance claims, and another's job is to obtain money from secondary insurance carriers who are supposed to pay some costs not authorized by Medicare. The two specialists may come to different opinions about a disputed claim based on differences in the rules of the two systems they represent.

Another example comes from public education. A high school coach has ties with an alumni organization that is pressuring for more emphasis on sports. The coach wants a shorter school day to allow more time for practice. However, a counselor in the school, who is working with parents concerned about the way their children are performing academically, is lobbying for a longer school day. One way organizations cope with potential conflicts such as this is by segregating specialists in different units. Another is to rotate the responsibilities.

Technology. Segal (1974) speculates that technology also can influence an organization's relationship with the environment. He distinguishes between so-called "chain-structured" and "mediative" technologies.

Chain-Structured Technologies. This type of technology consists of routinized, sequenced tasks. Relationships with the environment are channeled to focal points (i.e., persons, offices, departments). Each specialist is responsible for a selected aspect of the total environment. Consequently, during a hospital stay, a patient may visit an admissions office, one or more medical wards, a surgery ward, several diagnostic areas and clinics, and, of course, the billing department.

Mediative Technologies. With the mediative type of technology, specialized units are assigned responsibilities that require the worker to use discretion in settling assorted nonuniform problems. For instance, dissatisfied customers are referred to a service department staffed by personnel trained to deal with various types of complaints. In programs that compensate individuals for the costs of social disability or unemployment, specialized units have been set up, whose job is to match eligibility criteria with various client problems. The solutions depend heavily upon human judgment.

It is difficult to assess the efficiency of mediative organizations because there is no clear connection between the number of clients treated and the outcomes. For example, trends in welfare roles have no clear implication for the effectiveness of welfare agencies.

Network Structure

Important dimensions of network structures include patterns of ties, staking out organizational domains, and domain consensus.

Ties among Organizations. There are two fundamentally different ways to link organizations. One type of structure is *structural equivalence* (Burt, 1977; Laumann and Knoke, 1987: 12). It takes effect when two actors have similar ties with other members of a domain, regardless of their ties to each other. The other type of structure is called *subgroup cohesion.* Members of a cohesive network maintain dense mutual relationships with one another. Maximally connected subsets form "cliques," and overlapping cliques form "social circles."

Interdependence and Competition. *Interdependence,* sometimes called resource dependence, exists whenever one actor does not control the conditions necessary to achieve what it wants to accomplish (Pfeffer, 1982). When organizations rely on a common resource base, they necessarily become interdependent. Patterns of interdependence within a network provide keys to the way it functions. For example, since scarcity of resources promotes intense competition and rivalry, coordinating agencies are commonly used to regulate competition under conditions of scarcity (Litwak and Hylton, 1962).

When organizations have alternate suppliers, they can act more independently. Lazarsfeld and Thielens (1958) found that privately endowed colleges having independent sources of funding were less intimidated by pressure from politicians and trustees than were tax-supported institutions. Those which relied heavily on donations from a specific church were more vulnerable to external pressures than were large endowed colleges which drew their funds from many different donors.

Domain. The *domain* of an organization is defined by the overlap of its products and services with other organizations in the network (Levine, White, and Paul, 1963). For example, within the health field, the diseases a hospital covers, the populations it serves, and the services it renders determine its domain (Levine and White, 1961). The domain for a children's hospital is distinct from a nursing home because they provide dissimilar services to distinctive populations. A general hospital's domain overlaps the other two in that it serves both clienteles. However, in recognition of their distinctive domains, it may transport or refer patients to either of the other two hospitals. A similar idea can be stated more abstractly as follows: domain is defined by mutually relevant actions among actors in a substantive area (Laumann and Knoke, 1987: 9–10). Organizations that take one another's actions into account are part of the same domain (p. 11).

Virtually everything an organization does is dictated or shaped by its domain. It defines the products and services produced and the appropriate market and marketing strategies, and it determines how much competition will be encountered. Domain establishes an organization's status in an interorganizational network, regulating access to necessary resources and its right to operate in a given geographical area (Levine and White, 1961). It is, therefore, axiomatic that an organization will always act to define and preserve its domain (Warren, 1967). Since domains set constraints on size and function, organizations often act to expand their domains as well.

Because domains are so important, Warren (1967) postulates that organizations voluntarily collaborate only when it helps them preserve or expand their respective domains. In this regard, Meyer (1979), based on a study of 227 finance agencies of city, county, and state governments, suggested that an organization's intangible claims to a domain affect whether it is inclined to expand or contract responsibilities. Just as a type of organization (e.g., a cancer hospital) has a domain, so do entire networks have domains. For example, the health care field consists of hospitals, medical schools, pharmaceutical companies, and the like. Its functions parallel, and sometimes overlap, social services, which is comprised of a different set of organizations, such as adoption agencies, school social workers, and welfare offices.

Domain Consensus. *Domain consensus* refers to whether organizations accept one another's claims to a specific territory or clientele. Ability to reach a consensus on domains will tend to increase with the experience of constituent organizations. Conversely, domain boundaries will be especially problematic for a new organization. For a new organization, the wider its claims, the more likely it is to run up against vested interests opposed to its expansion (Evan, 1972). Once a consensus has been reached, competition declines because distributing resources among constituent organizations becomes a matter of routine.

Contextual Conditions

By "context," here, we mean characteristics associated with networks that are not inherent in either internal structures of the constituent organizations or direct relationships among network partners. Three will be mentioned: network size, environmental stability, and community/regional structure.

Size of Network. The types of relationships that form within a network depend on the number of constituent organizations. For example, the more organizations that are involved, the greater the *diversity* in the kinds of relationships that will be formed. In a diverse network, some organizations will be in competition. Others will find common interests and enter into coalitions. Still others relate only indirectly.

Size also helps determine whether a *coordinating agency* is needed, and it dictates the *density* of relationships that will form. The larger a network, the more organizations a given member potentially can interact with. Conversely, in a small network, the size sets a ceiling on the number of possible partners. The fewer the partners, the more frequently they will associate (see also, Granovetter, 1973).

Evan (1972) hypothesized that network size is correlated with the *autonomy* of the constituent organizations. In large networks, dependencies are spread among partners, giving each organization more choice, and consequently more autonomy. Burt found that profits of establishments vary with the structure of autonomy within a field (1983a: 13). Profits increase when competition among them is low and competition between suppliers is high. They decline when the bulk of buying and selling is with establishments that cooperate sufficiently to pursue collective interests.

Stability of the Environment. Terreberry (1968) maintained that in stable environments, the fate of one organization correlates inversely with the fate of another. This defines a pure state of competition in that this situation discourages any kind of cooperation. In a dynamic environment (e.g., during a natural disaster), on the other hand, organizations must depend more on one another and are, therefore, more likely to form networks.

Community and Regional Structure. The structure of local communities and regions also influences networking patterns. Turk (1977) examined the proposition that an integrated social setting affects the formation of new interorganizational activities and arrangements. He used the number of national headquarters located in a city as an index of its integration into the broader society. To estimate local integration, he used the number of community-wide associations. He reported finding an inverse relationship between local integration and extralocal integration. In other words, cities with many organizational ties to the national society had fewer community-wide associations, and vice versa.

Attempting to predict the occurrence of hospital councils within 130 large U.S. cities, Turk then found that they were more likely to form in the largest cities, and those with the most diversified municipal governments, than elsewhere. He used city size as an indicator of the number of municipal employees. Per capita expenditures in seven different areas were used to assess diversification.

SUMMARY AND CONCLUSIONS

Since organizations are not self-sufficient, they form networks of alliances, which, in turn, spin off webs of cooperation, negotiation, competition, and conflict. In this chapter, we reviewed some principles underlying those relationships. A *network,* we agreed, is a specific social structure consisting of all connected relationships among affiliated collectivities. Since network partners are often indirectly connected through third parties, they are not always aware of one another. Indirect relationships are based on more complex and abstract expectations than are direct relationships.

For research purposes, it is usually advisable to distinguish lateral networks from organizational sets. Both types can be studied in one of two ways—either by concentrating on a specific organization (a focal perspective), or by mapping patterns formed by the overall network (a global perspective). When one studies a focal organization, it is important to consider that some use more boundary specialists than others, because the focus always is on the linkages between it and the partners. On the other hand, a global perspective directs the investigator to map broad patterns among constituent organizations, such as forms of interdependence, authority patterns, and division of labor within a network. For example, the global view tell us that for a given level of resources, relationships within lateral networks are likely to be less competitive (and more symbiotic) than in an organization set.

We discussed forms of dependence, structural patterns within a network, mechanisms linking organizations, and organizational boundaries. Several reasons were found to account for the formation of networks and differences in network patterns. For example, relationships among organizations are dictated by their separate authority hierarchies, division of labor, roles, rules, and technologies. Structures such as these buffer the impact of other organizations. Other important factors include the level of consensus and competition among constituent organizations, overlap in their domains, size of the network, amount of turbulence in the environment, and community and regional structure.

There is a systematic relationship between the incentives for forming a network and its characteristic structure. We proposed that coercive relationships predominate in corporate structures; exchange relationships govern federative structures; and normative incentives are the basis of coalitional structures.

In this chapter, our focus has been on relationships within networks. However, we should emphasize that, from our theoretical perspective, these patterns are of little interest unless they affect network outcomes (i.e., the goods and services a network produces). We believe that the output of the organizations within a network will be directly and indirectly affected by many of the properties we have considered in this chapter. In the following chapters, our focus will be kept more steadfastly to this concern we have about the output.

NOTES

1. Because it minimizes predictability and expends resources, thus promoting accommodations reflected in new divisions of labor, clarification of domains, and the like (Levine and White, 1961).

CHAPTER 5

Individualistic Theories
of Earnings

Earlier, we faulted organizational ecology for failing to consider whether an organization's survival might affect outcomes that make any difference to the society. We advocated network models because they can be used to trace outcomes back to dependencies among the organizations that produce them. In this chapter and the next, we shall consider how organizational networks produce one kind of outcome, namely, the distribution of income within a society. The question to be addressed is this: *Why do individual earnings differ?*

OVERVIEW

Numerous writers have tackled this question in various ways. However, the answers have been disappointing. Most explanations we have found, in one way or another, are preoccupied with individuals. Furthermore, in nearly all prevailing accounts, individuals are regarded as disconnected beings and treated as independent events within ubiquitous regression models. Some of this work will be reviewed in this chapter. Then, in Chapter 6 we will take a different tack. We develop the position that personal income can be explained as an outcome of career patterns formed among interdependent work organizations. Therefore, we maintain, the explanation of personal income must focus on the interdependencies among work organizations.

Ways to Explain Income Distributions

The frequency distributions of earnings in all industrially advanced countries are skewed in a positive direction. However, when plotted, the logarithm of the earnings distribution is nearly symmetrical. Lyndall (1968) concluded that the central part of the distribution is close to lognormal, but the upper tail approaches a Pareto distribution. Economists and sociologists have tried to explain this pattern in an assortment of ways, with varying degrees of success. We have grouped them as follows:[1]

1. Choice theories
2. Characteristics theories
3. Job structure theories
4. Labor market theories
5. Career network theories
6. Interorganization income transfer theories

Of course, these approaches are not all mutually exclusive. For example, abilities and educational qualifications, which are used in characteristics theories, can be included in job structure explanations as well. Nevertheless, there are fundamental differences in the underlying suppositions:

- The first two theories attribute income to traits of individuals, or the things they do. They are the subject of this chapter.
- The others impute personal income to the way work is organized.

The last two theories have barely been mentioned in the literature. However, we believe they go to the crux of the issue more effectively than any of the others. This theme will be developed in the following chapter.

CHOICE THEORIES

Some economists regard economics as the "science of choices" and, therefore, hold that choice theories are the only valid economic theories of income distribution. The so-called human capital theory reigns supreme among this type of theory. Becker sees it as "the means of bringing the theory of personal income distribution back into economics" (1964: 66). Mincer (1970; 1974; 1976) and Chiswick (1974) have provided excellent expositions.

The Underlying Assumptions

Sociologists have usually relied on regression techniques to account for variance in income. Such techniques are directly or indirectly based on human resource labor market models.

Regression Techniques. To use regression models appropriately, the investigator must make the following assumptions:

- Wages reflect an individual status attainment, which is a straight-forward exchange of wages for skills.
- Workers act independently and compete with all other workers for the highest wage; employers compete for desired skills by meeting the current wage rates.
- Pay is the mechanism responsible for attracting the most competent individuals to some jobs and allocating the less competent to others.
- Employees can increase earnings only by improving their skills and performance.
- Consequently, job recruitment and retention must be explained by the career biographies of individuals; status differences, it is presumed, reflect variations in personal attributes, chances, and abilities.

Human Capital Theory. Human capital theory is associated with Nobel Prize winner Gary S. Becker, professor of economics and sociology at the University of Chicago. Each person's human capital consists of the skills and abilities acquired due to investments they make in themselves through education and training. The idea is used to explain why some occupations pay more than others. For example, physicians make more money than garbage collectors because they have acquired more education as a prerequisite for entering the occupation. According to the theory, an individual's earnings depend upon

- the earnings he (she) would receive without any training,
- dollars invested in training (i.e., years of formal education completed and years of labor market experience), and
- rate of return received from the investment in education.

The following simplifying assumptions underlay the theory:

- Everyone can choose freely among occupations without fear of discrimination.
- There are no inequalities in intelligence of people, their physical skills, home background, and the like.
- Any person can borrow money on the same terms as any other.
- Occupations differ in the length of training required.

Just as Adam Smith said, under these conditions occupations requiring longer periods of training will be forced to provide correspondingly higher levels of earnings to attract workers. Conversely, people invest in training to enter the occupation of their choice. Presumably, this choice is based on the length of education compared to the current value of the stream of earnings wanted over their lifetime. The stream has to be discounted, however, because over time, the value of earnings depreciates with inflation.

Formal Expressions of the Model

For the moment, we shall confine our attention to formal schooling. The above assumptions can be expressed formally as follows. Suppose a person without any formal education earns E_0 every year. Assume that

- during the years a person attends school, he (she) has no earnings, that is, one "invests" in education one's entire potential earnings while enrolled in school.
- immediately after school, the person enters the labor force.

Then, a person with one year of education earns nothing during the first year and $E_0 (1 + r)$ during each subsequent year. The r stands for rate of return on his (her) investment, which is assumed time-invariant. A person with two years of education earns nothing during the first two years and $E_0 (1 + r)^2$ during each subsequent year.

In general, a person with S years of education earns nothing during the first S years, and

$$E_s = E_0 (1 + r)^s \tag{1}$$

during each subsequent year. If the rate of return were not time-invariant, formula (1) becomes

$$E_s = E_0 (1 + r_1) (1 + r_2) \ldots (1 + r_s) \tag{2}$$

Now we can make the formula more realistic. Assume the investment in education is a fraction of the potential earnings each year. Thus, if a person with no education earns E_0, then another with just one year of education, during each year after the first, earns

$$E_1 = E_0 + r_1 (K_1 E_0) = E_0 (1 + r_1 K_1) \tag{3}$$

The expression $K_1 E_0$ is the investment in education during the first year. In general a person with S years of education earns

$$E_s = E_0 (1 + r_1 K_1) (1 + r_2 K_2) \ldots (1 + r_s K_s) \tag{4}$$

in each year after school. With logarithms, we can use the approximation $\log (1 + x) = x$. When x is small, we obtain from equation (4)

$$\log E_s = \log E_0 + r_1 K_1 + \ldots + r_s K_s \qquad (5)$$

Coupled with the assumption of equal opportunities, equation (5) describes the distribution of earnings.

Thus, from the simplifying assumptions enumerated above, the explanation of earnings differentials lies in the differences in training required for different occupations. Everyone is equally well off in terms of the discounted current value of lifetime earnings.

Years of Work Experience. The simplifying assumptions are unrealistic, however. Accordingly, only a modest portion of the variance in individual earnings has been accounted for by this model (see, for example, Mincer, 1970; 1974). In recognition of this shortcoming, human capital theorists have shifted their attention to the influence of on-the-job training. Mincer observes that

An important source of earnings differentials among people who have completed the same level of education is age or the amount of time already spent in employment.... The profiles ... are subject to explanation by the same human capital framework.... (1980; 106)

Mincer and others have followed the strategy of representing the impact of on-the-job training by adding a mathematical function (typically quadratic) of work experience (EXP) to the right-hand side of (5). This yields

$$\log E_s = \log E_0 + (r_1 K_1 + r_2 K_2 + \ldots) + a\, \text{EXP} - b\, (\text{EXP})2 \qquad (6)$$

According to this model, at first, earnings rise as work experience (EXP) increases. The increase could, for example, reflect increased productivity due to learning during the early work experience. It reaches a maximum and then declines. Reduced productivity due to obsolescence and declining commitment over time accounts for part of the decline.

Age versus Work Experience. It is important to recognize that age and work experience are not identical because age = experience + age at leaving school. Mincer and others have found that when the variable, "years of work experience," is included in the model, the proportion of variance in individual earnings accounted for substantial increases. One analysis was based on a large sample (drawn from the 1960 U.S. Census of Population) consisting of white urban nonfarm and nonstudent males of age up to 65 years. Years of schooling alone accounted for only 7 percent of the variance of the logarithm of 1959 annual earnings. However, when years of work experience were included, the proportion of variance accounted for increases to 30 percent (Mincer, 1974: 92).

Reservations

Despite a large literature on choice theories, not all economists agree that human capital theory is better than competing theories. For example, consider Lyndall's (1979: 241–246) comments outlined below.

Beginning Wages as Opportunity Costs

The human capital theorists assume that there is a cost for on-the-job experience, most of which is borne by the worker by working for lower wages initially. This cost, however, is not an outlay. It is treated as an opportunity cost in that, while obtaining experience the worker foregoes opportunities for higher earnings in jobs requiring less experience.

There is a problem with this assumption. Since most jobs offer comparable opportunities to obtain experience, it is unrealistic to speak of opportunity costs. If there are no differences in the available "opportunities," how can there be opportunity costs?

Human capital theorists ignore this question. Whereas the options for advancement could be narrow in the first years, they assume workers have to pay for experience with lower beginning wages.

Even so, it is not realistic to assume, as Mincer (1974: 49) does, that the whole difference between a beginner's earnings and the earnings level achieved after about eight years of work measures the opportunity cost of work experience in the first year.

Capacity to Learn versus Experience

The essence of education is that it creates in the individual a capacity to learn. Up to a point and on average, people with advanced education can absorb technical instruction and general information used for their work more quickly than those with less education.

If this is true, it becomes nearly impossible to disentangle whether the earnings of entry-level workers are being affected by education or by the initial experience. However, some human capital theorists (e.g., Mincer) have decided to attribute rapid increases in productivity during the early career to the person's prior education, thus denying the importance of early experience.

Freedom to Choose

Human capital theory assumes that each person has perfect freedom to choose from among all possible careers; presumably, the person has perfect knowledge and operates in a flawless capital market.

Human capital theory is an interesting deductive exercise suitable for a hypothetical world. However, its applicability to real labor markets, which are governed by discrimination, secrecy, and personal connections, is dubious.

Earnings as an Investment in Education

Lifetime earnings offered by an occupation will not be much higher than the amount needed to repay the costs of prerequisite education and training at some normal rate of interest.

This assumption also is misleading because in practice, the supply/demand ratio can be distorted. Earnings often exceed the level required to compensate for prior education and training costs for several reasons, including these:

- First, in some occupations such as professional sports, productivity is especially responsive to abilities irrespective of education.
- Second, there are severe entry restrictions for some occupations, which limit the labor pool. For example, medical schools and crafts restrict admissions and apprenticeships, forcing wages up.
- Third, technical characteristics of the occupation dictate the length of time and volume of investment required for obtaining the requisite qualifications (i.e., education and training).

Implications. In short, the labor market does not operate in the smooth, perfectly competitive way posited by the human capital theory. Acknowledging this, some of its proponents have suggested modifications to consider other factors, such as the following:

- differences in working life due to mortality and early retirement;
- costs associated with training, such as fees, books, travel, and the like;
- student grants that reduce the cost of education; and
- expected rate of unemployment.

Becker (1964) even suggested that exogenously given distributions of "abilities" and "opportunities" should be included in the model.

These modifications would add realism to the human capital theory. However, they would distort the original thrust of the idea so much that it no longer would be a rational-choice explanation. Therefore, we turn to another widely used option.

CHARACTERISTICS THEORIES

These theories emphasize personal traits and the restrictions a society places on an individual's choices. They are derived from the following assumptions:

- One's capacity to be productive depends upon both personal abilities and the available opportunities.
- Each person's earnings will reflect his (her) capacity to produce.
- Interaction between a person's biological properties and personal experiences and opportunities encountered throughout the lifetime nurtures abilities.
- Characteristics in the environment that are most influential include the family into which an individual is born, the kind of occupation chosen for first employment, and the type of school the child attends.

Some of these characteristics will be considered in more detail.

Family

Children cannot choose their families, yet the family's influence on the child's career is usually enormous. Therefore, models following this approach tend to be preoccupied with ascribed characteristics such as parents' education and income, race and ethnicity, and gender. All these variables have proven relationships to earnings. (For brief reviews of this vast literature, see Phelps Brown, 1977, Chapters 7 and 9; Davie, Butler, and Goldstein, 1972; and Corwin and Namboodiri, 1989.)

First Occupation

Most people know that occupations vary in earnings prospects. However, new workers cannot accurately forecast the prospects. Lyndall points out that an expanding enterprise gives new entrants considerable opportunities for promotion, whereas a stagnant firm does not. He further observes that

Since it is impossible for the new entrant to make accurate forecasts about the future expansion of each enterprise, there is a large element of luck in the ultimate outcome of his choice. (1979: 249)

Luck. To the extent luck dictates individual careers, models based in their personal characteristics seem doomed to low explanatory power; yet during the 1960s and 1970s, sociological research on stratification was dominated by this focus on individual-level status attainment process. Despite the effort that went into this type of research, the focus has not been very fruitful.

Schooling

If there is any hope of predicting an individual's occupational status attainment (and, therefore, income), it is through formal education. Several influential studies have concluded that the critical path to occupational status is through education and that it is the single most important determinant (Blau and Duncan, 1967; Featherman and Hauser, 1978; Sewell and Hauser, 1975; Alexander, Eckland, and Griffin, 1981).

Why Does Education Affect Occupational Status? Despite a widespread consensus on the importance of formal education, studies of income have failed to illuminate why people who stay in school earn more money. Nearly all studies have used the variable, "number of years of schooling completed," as a proxy for education. The results have not thrown much light on the status attainment process, notwithstanding uniformly high correlations with income. The problem is that this measure does not tell us anything about what happens in schools and colleges that could account for the benefits enjoyed by those who attend.

Several possible reasons can be imagined to explain why schooling pays off. However, since researchers are not paying attention to this question, their relative importance has not been sorted out. Is the decisive factor the general knowledge that students might have acquired? Or, perhaps, critical technical abilities they mastered? Students also learn valuable interpersonal skills, and they make social contacts in schools and colleges (see Corwin, 1986; Corwin and Namboodiri, 1989; Drebeen, 1968). Then, too, employers supposedly prefer workers who have developed good work habits, manners, discipline, and the like. Schools and colleges reward and encourage various forms of conformity. Such skills seem especially appropriate for "bureaucratic and hierarchical" organizations (Gintis, 1971; Lyndall, 1979: 248).

It is also possible that the relationship is only an illusion. Perhaps formal education masks other personal characteristics that make a person successful in both school and work. For example, the people who stay in school longer might also have more intellectual ability and more advantageous family backgrounds and cultural interests.

School Effects. What *is* known is that certain qualities of schools affect children's attitudes, habits, behavior, and abilities (see, for example, Psacharopoulos, 1975, for a summary of the relevant statistical evidence). It is also known that schools affect life chances through allocation practices they use, such as grade-promotion policies, tracking, and sponsorship. Warner, Havighurst, and Loeb likened schools to "enormous, complicated machine[s] for sorting and ticketing and routing children through life" (1944: 49).

More research is needed to find out what goes on in schools that might account for the correlation between years of education and income (see, especially, Corwin and Namboodiri, 1989; and Kerckhoff, 1976). Research should be designed to trace a person's earnings in the work place back to practices used by his or her school—practices such as these:

- Grouping and tracking policies.
- Availability of specialized personnel and facilities.
- The amount of decision-making power exercised by administrators, the teachers, and parents.
- Grading, homework, and promotion policies.
- Curriculum structure and how courses are chosen.
- Student participation in extracurricular activities.
- Disciplinary practices.

Investigators typically use years of formal schooling as a substitute for a large portfolio of practices and procedures that schools customarily use. This convention only masks underlying relationships that may be involved. Years in school may account for variance in earnings models, but that is not the same thing as an explanation. Clearly, research will be unable to explain income differences until investigators find out more about how high schools, vocational schools, colleges, and graduate schools operate. Neglecting the critical organizational dimensions of the educational system, as usually has been the case, only prolongs the mystery surrounding high correlations between earnings and education.

We are not objecting, in principle, to the common practice of treating a school as a black box (see Chapter 1). It is not necessary to find out about everything that goes on in classrooms nor to link outcomes to social psychological processes. However, to rule out spurious correlations, one must be able to justify why a crucial relationship might exist, and this relationship is not very well understood. Relying exclusively on number of years in school only masks the central theoretical challenge and diverts research in an unproductive direction.

Analytic Approaches

Research on characteristics often proceeds, as we have been doing, by focusing on one variable at a time. Investigators use statistical models that allow them to identify and rank the relative importance of each variable. Once the relative importance has been established, the characteristics can be ranked in order of importance. In the simplest case, *all factors are assumed to operate at the same moment in time.* Thus, Atkinson has suggested a path model in which family background, ability, education and training, and chance are the determinants of earnings. In his model, the first two variables affect earnings both directly and indirectly through education and training (1983: 122).

As a rule, under the assumption just mentioned, the distribution of earnings will depend on (1) the distribution of each factor and (2) how the factors combine themselves to produce their total effect on earnings. For example, if all factors are normally distributed and if they combine linearly, that is,

$$y = b_0 + b_1 x_1 + \ldots + b_n x_n$$

where the term y is earnings and x_i $(i = 1, \ldots, n)$ is the value of factor i, then the distribution of y would be normal. Alternatively if the factors may combine themselves multiplicatively, such that

$$y = a g_1 \ldots g_n.$$

Where $g_i = x_i$ to the power of a parameter c_i $(i = 1, \ldots, n)$ and the factors are normally distributed, and noncorrelated, earnings would be distributed in a lognormal manner.

These equations can be made more realistic by adding two other refinements. First, assume that the total set of characteristics all interact so as to increase or decrease the importance of each characteristic in different ways. Then, the importance of a characteristic will depend on which other characteristics it is associated with, that is, the composition of the total set of characteristics. Second, assume that variables in a given set will not all have their primary effect at the same period in the life course. In recognition of this likelihood, the data should be lagged through time. One would then pinpoint the career stage at which family background variables begin to lose some of their power, at which age schooling variables have maximum effect, and when on-the-job training and experience are factors.

Data Required. Enormous amounts of data are required to fully explore the influence of the full spectrum of relevant characteristics on earnings. As Lyndall put it:

Ideally, one would need information from a large and representative sample of individuals, with measurements of their annual earnings, in several different years; demographic and health data; occupation, industry, and size of firm at different stages of life; parents' backgrounds and other characteristics; abilities of various sorts (not just IQ); quantity and quality of education; history of promotion opportunities and choices made; attitudes toward work; and willingness to work harder or accept greater responsibility for the sake of higher earnings. A sample which contained a large number of identical twins would also permit an analysis of genetic influences. . . . (1979: 250–251)

CONCLUSIONS

This chapter has confronted the question, why do individual earnings differ? We find that most explanations focus on individuals, who are, in turn, treated in regression models as independent of each other. In the next chapter, we shall argue for a different type of explanation, one based on organizational structure and network ties. In contrast to the individualistic approaches considered here, this approach explains personal income as an outcome of career patterns formed among interdependent work organizations. Therefore, we maintain, the explanation of personal income must focus on the interdependencies among work organizations.

This chapter has introduced the topic of earnings and provided some necessary background. Accordingly, we reviewed some popular individualistic theories of earnings. The human capital theory explains income differences in terms of a person's acquired skills and abilities, which he or she possesses because of investments made through education and training. Occupations requiring more training will be forced to provide correspondingly higher levels of earnings to attract workers. Conversely, people invest in training with a view to entering the occupation of their choice.

It soon became clear that several assumptions would have to be added to the model to make it more realistic. Even so, we must conclude that, while the human capital theory is an interesting deductive exercise suitable for a hypothetical world, it has only limited applicability to real labor markets, which are driven by discrimination, secrecy, and personal connections. In particular, it is not realistic to assume that the entire difference between a beginner's earnings and his income about eight years later somehow reflects opportunity costs foregone during the first year. If one were to make the modifications necessary to make the model realistic, it would distort the theory so much that it could no longer qualify as a pure rational-choice explanation.

Another individualistic approach concentrates on how an individual's personal attributes and social situation affect that person's earnings. Characteristic theories are concerned about how a person's attributes and social conditions he or she is confronting limit his or her choices. Perhaps the single most powerful personal characteristic influencing income is years of formal education a person has completed.

However, despite a widespread consensus on the importance of formal education, studies of personal earnings have failed to illuminate why education brings higher income. We know that it has something to do with certain qualities of schools, which can affect children's attitudes, habits, behavior, and abilities. Therefore, more research is needed to find out what actually goes on in schools, colleges, and vocational training centers that might account for the correlation between years of education and income. Neglecting the critical organizational dimensions of the educational system, as social scientists have been doing, only prolongs the mystery surrounding high correlations between earnings and education.

Investigators who study characteristics often use statistical models that allow them to identify the relative importance of each variable. Once this has been established, the characteristics can be ranked in order of importance. However, since characteristics do not function independently, simultaneous effects models are can be useful. When there are simultaneous effects, the distribution of earnings will depend on (1) the distribution of each factor and (2) how the factors combine themselves to produce their total effect on earnings. As a necessary refinement, changes should be tracked over time. However, one needs enormous amounts of data to fully explore the influence of the full spectrum of relevant characteristics on earnings.

NOTE

1. We have not included in this grouping stochastic theories, since they do not address the economic process that generates income distribution. They are instead designed to capture empirical regularities, such as the shape of the distribution. Gibrat (1931) derived the lognormal distribution from the "law of proportional effect" reflected in the relationship

$$y_t = y_{t-1} (1 + u_t). \tag{1}$$

The expression y_g is income in period g ($g = t, t-1$). The expression u_t is a normally distributed random variable. We can assume the following relationship between y_t and y_{t-1}

$$y_t = y_{t-1} + u_t. \tag{2}$$

The term u_t is a component drawn at random from a normal distribution with mean 0 and standard deviation sigma. If this "law" remains unchanged for a long time in a population, then the earnings distribution in that population will be normal. If instead of actual earnings y stands for the logarithm of earnings, then process (2) described above will generate a lognormal distribution. If u_t is drawn from a normal distribution with mean less than zero and there is a lower bound to the level of earnings, then process (2) will generate a Pareto

CHAPTER 6

Structural and Network
Theories of Earnings

The discussion of income, introduced in the previous chapter, now takes a sharp turn toward structural types of theories. Five will be considered in this chapter: job structures, organized labor, labor markets, career networks, and interorganization income transfers. We shall start here with theories about how job structures influence individual earnings.

OVERVIEW

The theories considered in the last chapter, which concentrate on individual choice mechanisms and personal characteristics, account for only the supply side of the earnings equation. However, earnings depend largely on the level of demand for different types of workers. Demand fluctuates with the industry and workplace structure, and several other conditions. Consequently, a group of people who work in diverse settings can have identical personal characteristics and, yet, not have the same incomes due to differences in their work settings.

Some crucial demand characteristics have been uncovered in several studies. Of special importance are characteristics of firms, companies, corporations, factories, and other work places; unionization; type of industry and the occupations represented in it; region of the country; and the labor markets themselves. Wachtel and Betsy (1972) found that many characteristics of this kind affect individual earnings to a significant degree—far more than the effects of personal characteristics that are customarily used to explain income, such as education, years in the present job, race, sex, age, and marital status (see also Rees and Schultz, 1970).

Attributes of Individuals versus Structural Explanations

Structural divisions within factories were central to Marx's class model. Still, for a long time, sociologists disregarded variations in the very work places that are most responsible for workers' incomes. Stratification research in the 1950s and 1960s convoluted into mutual admiration ratings inspired by Warner's *Index of Status Characteristics*. The purpose of this research was to rank individuals within a community based on their prestige ratings and status characteristics. Blau and Duncan's (1967) landmark status attainment study returned to questions with profound structural implications. They were concerned about whether class boundaries are being eroded by universalistic standards spread through industrialization; that is, is social mobility increasing? However, their data consisted of correlations among the status attributes of individuals, not the attributes of their work places.

In arresting contrast, structural theories credit workers' incomes to the wage policies of large, powerful corporations and public bureacracies. Seniority systems and elaborate rules governing promotions and salaries help insulate these organizations from conventional economic market forces. A worker only needs to perform at minimum levels, since wages are tied to jobs, not to exceptional performance in comparison to other workers. Beyond the way work places are themselves organized, one must consider an equally fundamental dimension. They are typically linked together, formally and informally, in such a way as to form career ladders. Socially mobile workers increase their incomes by moving systematically from one place of employment to another.

JOB STRUCTURE THEORIES

There is growing evidence that income differences can be accounted for by size of firm, authority structure, work structure, and organized labor (cf. Baron and Bielby, 1984; Stewman and Konda, 1983: 638). In addition, we propose that incomes depend on distributions of vacancies that ripple through networks of interconnected work organizations.

Wage Differences between Firms

From a practical standpoint, demand for different types of workers is most visibly reflected in the structure of job opportunities. Opportunities are, in turn, governed by pay levels attached to job titles. Douty found that much of the difference in factory wages can be accounted for by differences in wage levels between plants. He concluded that "the findings confirm the widespread impression of the existence within labor markets of a hierarchy of wage levels among firms" (1961: 72). This raises the question, which features of work organizations are responsible for interfirm differences? There are many possible answers, including region of the country, size of the firm, and its authority structure.

Size of Firm. It is well documented that the size of an employing organization is positively correlated with its wage rates, because large employers have proportionately more well-paid specialists and managers. That is not all, though. In addition, other workers tend to be paid better than comparable workers in smaller firms. Lyndall (1968) suggested that since big companies are capital intensive, employees usually work with expensive equipment. High wages are their rewards for using it efficiently.

Authority Structure. Simon (1957) observed that the salary of an executive is a constant multiple of that person's subordinates. The resulting distribution of salaries turns out to be of the Pareto form. Sociologists have been investigating the effects of authority structures on incomes for some time (see, especially, Wright and Perrone, 1977; Robinson and Kelley, 1979). Spaeth postulates that jobs that provide control over other personnel and over money are more critical and that, consequently, they pay more. His data show that

among men, control over monetary resources is a stronger determinant of earnings than other work-related variables. Among women, control over monetary resources and control over personnel are jointly stronger determinants of earnings than other work related variables. (1985: 603)

Other work-related variables that were in his equation explained less of the variance. Still, it is worth noting that (1) number of management levels, (2) amount of authority exercised, (3) supervisory responsibility, and, for men, (4) discretion all made statistically significant contributions to earnings.

Wage Hierarchies within Firms

It is impossible to understand wage hierarchies between firms without considering wage hierarchies within firms. Together, the two types of wage hierarchies make up an *organizational labor market*. The availability of skilled workers, pay levels, and prospects for promotion may be called *job distribution* (Thurow, 1976), or *job structure* (Lyndall, 1979: 257).

Internal Labor Markets. Thurow and Lucas advanced the thesis that

Wages are paid based on the characteristics of the job in question, and workers are distributed across job opportunities based on their relative position in the labor queue. (1972: 172)

Major organizations are bureaucratized. Elaborate rules and procedures, such as labor contracts and seniority provisions, govern access to jobs and wages. Thus, many studies have concentrated on identifying specific characteristics of jobs that can significantly affect wages.

Doeringer and Piore (1971) called attention to the fact that employment within work organizations is, to a large degree, insulated from the outside labor market. Jobs are arranged hierarchically, and entry from outside is limited to mainly lower levels. Vacancies at other levels are filled by promotions or transfers from within. Job security and predictable chances for advancement make this arrangement attractive to employees and labor unions. They called such an arrangement an *internal labor market.*

Employers expect their employees to improve their skills through on-the-job training. Recruiters consider an outside applicant's chances of learning to become a productive worker. Thus, individuals with identical backgrounds may end on different earnings trajectories, depending upon the indicators employers use to screen applicants and the types of training they provide.

Types of Job Hierarchies. Two types of job hierarchies have been distinguished: *technical interdependence* and *career trajectories* (Sorenson and Kalleberg, 1981).

Technical Interdependence. The first type, technical interdependence, is present when one job cannot be accomplished without the others. When interdependence is high, the interconnectedness among apparently different jobs makes it difficult to measure and reward individual contributions to collective outcomes.

Career Trajectories. In the second type of hierarchy, rules (not mutual dependence) are used to link jobs to each other. Acceptable performance in one job can be used as a stepping stone into another type of job only remotely connected to the first. The second job often requires entirely different skills. Job titles are arranged in orderly patterns, which form "lifetime careers," that is, "a succession of related jobs, arranged in a hierarchy of prestige, through which persons move in an orderly, and predictable sequence" (Wilensky, 1960).

Micro Structures. Job hierarchies can be broken down into several micro structures and related processes. Micro structures consist of the following:

- *Grade distributions:* the number of echelons and the percentage of workers represented at each level of authority (e.g., percent in managerial positions);
- *Grade ratios:* the number in a rank compared to the number in the next highest rank (e.g., number of school principals compared to number of school teachers);

- *Vacancy chains:* the number of positions available at each rank as determined by (a) the organization's rate of growth or decline, (b) exits, and (c) openings created by promotions at higher levels;
- *Cohort size:* number and mix of potential competitors having the preferred characteristics; and
- *Personnel policies:* priority that managers give to factors such as seniority, formal education, skills, and the like. (see, especially, Stewman and Konda, 1983)

It is important to observe that an individual's career will be shaped not only by opportunities within that person's own organization but also by how fast organizations within the relevant network are growing or declining. Expansion and contraction throughout the network of affiliated organizations will affect both exit rates and promotion rates within each organization in the set.

Internal job hierarchies act as filters to opportunities in the network. Some positions, such as entry-level jobs, afford very little opportunity for promotion to a higher-paying position in another organization. Other positions, however, provide visibility and contacts with outside organizations. This is especially true of boundary roles. For example, a public affairs director of a college represents the college on many boards throughout the region and, in the process, becomes known to potential employers. Jobs that require travel to national meetings also present opportunities for contacts with potential employers. Thus, through these windows, internal job chains become linked with opportunities in still other organizations. Some jobs within the work organization open opportunities and act as stepping stones to jobs elsewhere. As an employee moves through various positions, outside opportunities open and close, depending on how they are connected to the network.

Caveats. It is clear, then, that characteristics of job hierarchies within organizations help explain part of the differences between them with respect to incomes earned by their employees. However, one must be cautious because the fit between job titles and income is not perfect. The match is complicated by

- variations among career patterns. Spilerman (1977) distinguishes between "orderly" and "chaotic" career lines. In the former, earnings and occupational prestige increase steadily over time. Chaotic career patterns have no such regularities. For example, the career profile of teachers is comparatively unstaged and "front-loaded." In other words, their beginning salary is high-level compared with their ultimate earning potential (see Lortie, 1975).
- trade-offs between money and other rewards, such as insurance benefits, prestige, and autonomy. For example, some school teachers sacrifice pay for

the intrinsic pleasure of working with children, for classroom autonomy, and for the opportunity to participate in decisions (see Chapman and Lowther, 1982).

- variations in the way internal labor markets work in different organizations. In many work places, labor turnover is high, and there is no provision for a lifetime career.
- effects of technological change. Tinbergen (1975) argued that changes in the relative earnings of graduates are outcomes of a "race" between the expansion of higher education and growth in demand arising from technological development.

THEORIES ABOUT ORGANIZED LABOR

Employees negotiate their wages, and labor unions affect those negotiations. It is reasonable to suppose a principal aim of any union is to maintain and, when possible, raise wages (Hunter and Robertson, 1969: 275).

Control over Labor Supply

The power of unions to influence wages stems from their ability to control the supply of labor. Older craft unions restricted it by placing limits on the number of apprenticeship programs that are permitted and controlling the workers' access to them.

Another way to gain power is to make union membership a condition of employment. In some circumstances, unions are known to have gained the right to nominate people to fill vacancies. Other forms of control are slowdowns and work stoppages (Atkinson, 1983: 132).

Power of Employers

Employers also adopt measures to improve their bargaining position through such avenues as employers' associations. They sometimes move to new locations where labor unions are weak, or avoid areas where they are strong. In any case, it is axiomatic that, individually and collectively, employers will use their power to limit the wages paid. Where labor is unorganized, this may lead to exploitation. Where labor unions are powerful, the wage levels will be decided by the relative bargaining strengths of the two sides.

Wages in Unionized and Non-Unionized Sectors

One might suppose that wages in the unionized sector would be higher than in non-unionized firms. However, it is not that simple because unionized wages can spill over into the non-unionized sector. For example, if unionized salaried employees (e.g., in the government sector) get a 4 percent raise, then employers with non-unionized employees might be compelled to give the same raise to compete for salaried workers. If there are no spill over effects, then the flow from the unionized sector to the non-unionized sector, and vice versa, can have a significant impact on distribution of earnings (see Mulvey, 1980).

Social scientists have studied the wage differentials between union and non-union companies extensively. Lewis (1963) investigated how unionization influenced earnings of different industries in the United States between 1920 and 1958. Also, Mulvey (1976) examined the effect of collective bargaining on relative earnings in U.K. manufacturing in 1973. Freeman (1980) found that in the United States, dispersion among unionized workers was considerably lower than among non-unionized workers. He also reported that the production worker/nonproduction worker differential within establishments narrowed because of unionization. Labor unions are known to insist on payment according to the same uniform standard (Webb and Webb, 1902). Of course, the impact of unionization on the complete earnings distribution depends upon whether the relative gains of union members are at the expense of non-union members or profits.

LABOR MARKET THEORIES

During the past decade, sociologists have devoted time and effort investigating how labor market composition affects incomes. Some properties often mentioned are (1) the role of custom and the emergence of new industries, (2) discrimination, and (3) segmentation.

Custom and New Industries

Wage rates are often based on custom. For example, police officers and fire fighters get the same salaries in the United States, even in the face of an oversupply of fire fighters and serious shortages of police (Phelps Brown, 1962; Doeringer and Piore, 1971).

Industries created during the early part of the industrial revolution, such as textiles and footwear, had to offer wage premiums to attract labor from agriculture. Each new industry has had to offer increasingly more attractive wages to attract employees, the newest industries paying the highest wages and other things being equal (Lutz, 1976: 473). Currently, when workers move from one firm to another, they usually receive a salary premium and other perquisites as incentives.

Discrimination

After reviewing two types of economic discrimination, we will consider how discrimination has been used to explain earnings.

Types of Economic Discrimination. Two main types of economic discrimination are distinguished in the literature: educational opportunities and employment–wage discrimination.

Discrimination in Educational Opportunity. This type of discrimination occurs before workers enter the labor market. The most tangible form is the lack of needed facilities and general inferiority of public schools that are available to minorities. Racial minorities endure cumulative educational handicaps beginning early in the schooling process. Accordingly, much of the disadvantage they experience in the marketplace can be attributed to

- inequitable distribution of resources to black and white neighborhoods within and between school districts;
- tracking systems, which disproportionately allocate Blacks to vocational programs;
- a control structure dominated by white families; and
- a sponsorship network that routinely excludes large numbers of black families.

Lieberson (1980) observes that during the 1920s and 1930s, when the white European groups were making their greatest strides in education, most Blacks were still located in poor, white-controlled Southern schools. These schools have been characteristically apathetic about requiring minority children to attend, and they are oriented predominantly to low-paying service and manual occupations.

Employment and Wage Discrimination. Employment discrimination refers to the practice of allocating women and minorities to the least desirable, worst-paying jobs, compared to jobs available to their counterparts with comparable education and training. Wage discrimination occurs when a group (e.g., Blacks) receives lower pay than another group for the same job.

Economic Explanations for Discrimination. The economic explanations for discrimination fall into three categories:

1. The so-called "power" explanation concentrates on the ability of powerful groups to gain economic benefits at the expense of other groups.
2. A more conventional explanation is based on "taste" factors. It holds that members of one group avoid associating with members of another group.
3. The third explanation is based on the notion that some employers use negative stereotypes about minorities in making hiring and promotion decisions.

Labor Market Segmentation

It is now generally recognized that firms in the core and periphery of the economy tend to have different management systems, promotion practices, and hiring policies. The distinction points to the fact that labor markets are segmented. Other typologies of economic segmentation, some more complex than others, subscribe to similar assumptions (Hodson and Kaufman, 1982).

Dual Economy. One often-cited distinction holds that the labor market is divided into two broad sectors, engendering a dual labor market. The *primary sector* is characterized by employment stability. Promotions take place among similar firms within the sector, and workers are well paid and rewarded for skill and experience. The *secondary sector* is a total contrast. It is characterized by unstable employment, low wages, lack of skills in the work force, and poor promotion opportunities.

Research on Industries. The exact unit that is supposedly "segmented" has never been clearly established, however. It has become almost standard practice to categorize entire industries into one or another segment. This approach produces grave ambiguities, because a so-called "industry" is an abstract label that encompasses many types of actual work organizations. Any industry includes diverse organizations that differ in size, structure, and occupational composition. For example, the manufacturing industry includes General Motors and small machine shops.

Research at the level of industries has not accounted for much of the difference in income. Moreover, explanations for identifiable differences among industries tend to be based on conjecture about presumed differences in the organizational characteristics of work places located in different segments of the economy. However, the correspondence is largely untested and loose at best.

Organizations versus Industries. In their provocative paper, Baron and Bielby make a convincing argument that investigators who have attempted to test segmentation perspectives often misspecify the problem because they neglect to sample characteristics of organizations. As they interpret their own data, differences between industries boil down to two dimensions: organizational structure (complexity) and centrality of organizations within exchange networks (dominance). They suggest the following:

Firms that dominate their environments or which are internally complex are more "top heavy," more closed off to external entrants, and have more of their jobs in career ladders. (1984: 468)

Furthermore, they conclude, the correlation between organizational segmentation and labor market segmentation is weak.

Organizations with a specific structure, technology, and scale occupy diverse niches and varied organizational types populate the same environment. (p. 471)

If employment practices dictate wages, it follows that work places, not industries, should be the primary sampling unit. A few studies devoted to this thesis reinforce the importance of organizational characteristics. For example:

- Hodson (1984) found that organization size is the most significant determinant of earnings at the company level.
- Another researcher concluded that the effect of schooling on earnings varies as a linear function of the logarithm of size of establishment (Stolzenberg, 1978: 825). He speculates that large employers prefer educated workers because they function better in a complex, standardized environment.
- Promotion opportunities are determined by the proportion of employees in supervisory positions, turnover rates at each level, and age distribution (Smith, 1979).
- Baron and Strang (1990) found, in this regard, that civil service divisions in California that were controlled by unions had unfavorable promotion opportunities as reflected in fewer vertical job titles.

Occupational Differences within Organizations. Doeringer and Piore (1971), who are usually credited for developing the notion of dual economy, had in mind differences between places of employment. In this respect, they anticipated Baron and Bielby and others who believe research must become more sharply focused on the properties of work organizations. If one follows this lead, it would mean dividing all employing organizations into two (or more) categories. One problem with that tack is that any given employer can be represented in more than one labor market. As Craig et al. (1982) pointed out, canteen workers who work in large establishments represent a mixed category. They are situated in a primary-type firm but are in an occupation that has all the characteristics of the secondary sector. For example, they are paid low wages and have poor promotion prospects, and they need little training and have no job security. Also, as Parcel and Sickmeier (1988) point out, administrative personnel in fast-food chains have all the characteristics associated with the primary labor market. However, employees in local establishments are in the secondary sector.

Given the complexity of modern work organizations, research must include their occupational structures. Some organizations are dominated by one or two occupations. However, most employ many, even dozens, of occupational groups having diverse characteristics. Measures of segmentation need to account for variations within as well as among work organizations.

In the next chapter, we shall meet another problem associated with the practice of classifying a given organization into only one category. Probably most work organizations provide more than one kind of product or service, which would place it in more than one classification of most typologies one can imagine. Therefore, there must be a way to take multiple outputs into account.

CAREER NETWORK THEORIES

In our opinion, the most fundamental property of labor markets has been overlooked in most of the burgeoning literature on the subject. As we see it, a labor market is composed of networks of relationships among work organizations. These networks include (1) groups of work places performing comparable functions, such as automobile factories, and (2) surveillance organizations that have a stake in the output, such as regulatory agencies and consumer groups. While little attention has been given to this interorganizational component, we shall argue that network relationships have at least as much effect on income distribution as does any characteristic so far considered. We will confine our attention here to what we are calling *feeder systems, stepping stones, vacancy distributions,* and *nested dependencies.*

Feeder Systems

Certain types of careers are based on well-known connections among hierarchies of related organizations. Sometimes the linkages are for malized, as in the case of feeder systems. A feeder system consists of two or more stratified layers of organizations that are connected to each other through formal ties. The higher layers dominate lower ones because they control resources, have higher prestige, and provide output in high demand. Upwardly mobile careers flow from the lower set to the parent organizations. Downwardly mobile careers are also channeled through the same routes via routine demotions.

For example, managers of major league baseball teams use minor league teams ("farm clubs") as a pool of skilled labor. Often, employees have to work in its branch offices or obtain similar experience elsewhere to become eligible for positions at the headquarters office.

Stepping Stones

Connections need not be formalized, however. Some organizations routinely use others as sources of labor supply. For example, Ivy League colleges frequently recruit faculty members from Big Ten universities and small colleges. Those faculty members at Ivy League colleges who are not promoted look to lesser schools for employment. In much the same way, school superintendents move in predictable ways from small to large districts within a state.

There is no official bond between television stations in the United States, but each station has rank within a definite status hierarchy. Its status is based largely on the size and wealth of the viewing audience, which are estimated from surveys circulated throughout the industry. The career of a television newscaster consists of a series of jobs, linked in predictable ways, through this hierarchy. On the other hand, secretaries working at television stations are not constrained to stay with television stations. They can increase their wages by going to work for an entirely different type of organization. Even here, however, local labor markets are stratified, at least to the extent that experience in specific types of organizations influences the worker's chances of ending at a given destination.

Employment agencies, universities, training centers, and similar organizations play pivotal roles, both in defining stepping stone patterns and then in controlling flows of personnel through the system. Some of these mediators, like schools, are *people-changing agencies* (or socializing agencies) charged with the responsibility for equipping people with skills and otherwise adapting them to fit into a given niche. Such agencies are usually connected with satellites, or regular customers. For example, some school districts hire all their teachers from one or two colleges, which cater to their needs. Other distribution agencies do not change the skills and behavior of workers. Instead, they classify both workers and employers and then, after a screening process, put them in contact. They can be classified as *people-processing agencies*. Employment agencies, university admissions offices, and similar oganizations are examples.

Vacancy Distributions

It is obvious that an individual's career is shaped by the type of vacancy chains that form within places of employment (White, 1970). Two other implications are worth stressing. First, each cohort within a set of work places has its own career pattern. The pattern consists of changing distributions of vacancies as they develop over an organization. Suppose, for example, we find that between time 1 and time 2, proportionately more members of cohort A than cohort B reach managerial positions. Through research, we might learn the difference is due to fluctuations in rates of growth in different parts of the organization and exits at each rank. These two variables can be used to describe the shapes of the two distributions. We can now account for the success or failure of individuals in terms of the attributes of their cohort. This approach differs radically from the characteristics approach outlined earlier, which attributes earnings entirely to personal traits.

Second, we can extend these observations beyond particular organizations to networks of organizations. In other words, career patterns vary with distributions of vacancies and exits within entire families of interdependent organizations. It is axiomatic that the distributions will assume different shapes from one network to another and from time to time.

Nested Dependencies

We observed in the previous chapter that the resources available to a given set of organizations will be partially or largely controlled by external networks of organizations that control and allocate resources. These dependencies necessarily affect workers' earnings. For example, school districts obtain about one-half of their money from state legislatures, which must set allocation priorities among competing demands from other state agencies. At the local level, school districts compete for scarce tax dollars with police and fire departments and other services. At the state level, they compete with public colleges and universities, which also depend on state allocations. The money available to pay teachers, therefore, will be determined by this complex and highly interdependent system of nested relationships.

More generally, we may say the earnings of teachers and administrators within school districts depend on events that take place in a larger system in which school districts are components. A wide spectrum of events might be involved, such as the fates of tax levies, state school board policies, community demand for particular types of services (e.g., counseling), population growth rates and migration patterns, school district consolidation policies and policies governing school size, and competition from other public agencies.

Note that, because of the kind of nesting described here, work organizations do not just compete with one another (for the resources needed to pay wages), as is assumed by the organizational ecology approach. That approach, the reader will recall, defines organizations as members of a population of similar organizations that are competing only among themselves. Our point is that competition cuts across larger spheres.

INTERORGANIZATION INCOME TRANSFER THEORIES

So far, we have concentrated on transfers of human personnel between work organizations. Conceivably, the same type of transfer process governs incomes as well. As we see it, income transfers follow the flow of inputs and outputs among organizations involved in economic exchanges.

Economic Flows

To illustrate what we have in mind, following Miyazawa (1976), imagine two sectors, one consisting of households and the other consisting of industries. The household sector is stratified into M income groups, and the industrial sector is stratified into N business groups. For simplicity, assume that each household has only one earner and that each business produces only one output.

Consider a simple case involving three business groups and two household strata (income groups). The flow matrix of outputs can be depicted as shown in Figure 6.1. The first row shows the flow of output of Business 1 to various destinations; its total output is x_1. Of this, z_{11} goes to that business itself, z_{12} to Business 2, and z_{13} to Business 3. C_{11} goes to Household stratum (income group) 1, C_{12} to Household stratum 2, and f_1 to other consumers. Similarly, the second and third rows, respectively, show the flow of output of Business 2 and Business 3 to various destinations. The fourth row shows business-specific inputs of labor (in terms of wages and salaries) from Household stratum 1, and the fifth row shows the corresponding inputs from Household stratum 2.

Flow Equations. The following set of flow equations describes the destination make up of outputs from the three business groups:

$$x_1 = z_{11} + z_{12} + z_{13} + C_{11} + C_{12} + f_1$$
$$x_2 = z_{21} + z_{22} + z_{23} + C_{21} + C_{22} + f_2$$
$$x_3 = z_{31} + z_{32} + z_{33} + C_{31} + C_{32} + f_3$$

As written, the equations contain no explicit reference to wages and salaries received by the various household strata nor the corresponding consumption coefficients (fraction of wages and salaries expended on consumption of each business's outputs). They also do not contain any explicit reference to the "value-added" ratios (wages and salaries per dollar value of output). To incorporate these parameters explicitly, we first write

$$C_{11} = C_{11} (W_{11} + W_{12} + W_{13})/W_{1+}$$

for the total income of Household stratum 1 (using the notation W_{1+} for $W_{11} + W_{12} + W_{13}$).

If the first, second, and third terms within the parentheses are multiplied and divided by x_1, x_2, and x_3, respectively, we obtain the equation,

$$C_{11} = g_{11} (x_1 v_{11} + x_2 v_{12} + x_3 v_{13}).$$

Figure 6.1
A Flow Table Involving Three Business Groups and Two Household Strata

	Business			Income Group		Other	Total
	1	2	3	1	2	Other	Total
Business 1	z_{11}	z_{12}	z_{13}	C_{11}	C_{12}	f_1	x^1
Business 2	z_{21}	z_{22}	z_{23}	C_{21}	C_{22}	f_2	x^2
Business 3	z_{31}	z_{32}	z_{33}	C_{31}	C_{33}	f_3	x^3
Income group 1	W_{11}	W_{12}	W_{13}				
Income group 2	W_{21}	W_{22}	W_{23}				

The terms in the equation are defined as follows:

- The expression $g_{11} = C_{11}/W_{1+}$ is the fraction of the income of Household stratum 1 expended on consumption of the output of Business 1.
- The expression $v_{11} = W_{11}/x_1$ is the value-added ratio (wages and salaries per dollar value of output) of Business 1.
- The expression $v_{12} = W_{12}/x_2$ is the value-added ratio of Business 2.
- The expression $v_{13} = W_{13}/x_3$ is the value-added ratio of Business 3.

Similarly,

$$C_{12} = g_{12} (x_1 v_{21} + x_2 v_{22} + x_3 v_{23})$$

If interbusiness flows are expressed in terms of the so-called input coefficients (i.e., $a_{11} = z_{11}/x_1$, $a_{12} = z_{12}/x_2$, and so on), the destination composition of the output of Business 1 can be expressed as follows:

$$x_1 = a_{11}x_1 + a_{12}x_2 + a_{13}x_3 + g_{11} (x_1 v_{11} + x_2 v_{12} + x_3 v_{13}) \\ + g_{12} (x_1 v_{21} + x_2 v_{22} + x_3 v_{23}) + f_1$$

or equivalently (by collecting coefficients of x_is on the left-hand side)

$$[1 - (a_{11} + g_{11}v_{11} + g_{12}v_{21})] x_1 - (a_{12} + g_{11}v_{12} + g_{12}v_{22}) x_2 \\ - (a_{13} + g_{11}v_{13} + g_{12}v_{23}) x_3 = f_1$$

The corresponding equations for Business group 2 and Business group 3 are:

$$- (a_{21} + g_{21}v_{11} + g_{22}v_{21})\, x_1$$
$$+ [1 - (a_{22} + g_{21}v_{12} + g_{22}v_{22})]\, x_2$$
$$- (a_{23} + g_{21}v_{13} + g_{22}v_{23})\, x_3 = f_2$$

and

$$- (a_{31} + g_{31}v_{11} + g_{32}v_{21})\, x_1$$
$$- (a_{32} + g_{31}v_{12} + g_{32}v_{22})\, x_2$$
$$+ [1 - (a_{33} + g_{31}v_{13} + g_{32}v_{23})]\, x_3 = f_3,$$

respectively.

Assume that the value-added ratios, the consumption coefficients, and the input coefficients are given (remain fixed). Then, the equations just written express the relationship between final demand (f_1, f_2, and f_3) and total outputs (x_1, x_2, and x_3) of the various industries. In other words, these equations, considered simultaneously, establish how the final demand determines the outputs of the various industries via interbusiness flows and induced household consumption.

Now consider for a moment a change in the final demand that calls for an increase in the outputs (x_1, x_2, and x_3). The increase in output of the industries produces a corresponding increase in the income (wage and salaries) of the households in various strata. This, in turn, produces an increase in the consumption pattern of the "affected" household strata. An increase in the consumption of any given household stratum (say, h) calls for a corresponding increase in the outputs of the various industries, which, in turn, produces, among other things, an increase in the income of households in strata other than h.

This set of equations illuminates the interconnections among incomes of different household strata. We have shown that it is possible to express them mathematically. In the standard theories of income dispersion, however, these interconnections have received no attention.

SUMMARY AND CONCLUSIONS

We have maintained throughout that what is most important about networks is their outcomes. Outcomes include the products and services provided, but there are many other consequences as well. In the last two chapters, we have concerned ourselves with a generally overlooked outcome, namely, producing an income distribution within a society. We have explored some old and new ways to answer a question that has been repeatedly addressed in the literature: Why do individual earnings differ? Our review in Chapter 5 shows that, during the 1970s, explanations were preoccupied with individuals and, furthermore, that the individuals were almost always treated as though they were independent of one another. However, we maintain that personal income is governed by interdependent networks of work organizations. The organizations are tied together in ways that produce career ladders. Workers make their way through webs of employers over their work life, not only by changing jobs but also by changing employers. The route is governed in part by complex job structures within employing firms. Some positions do not afford much opportunity to take better employment. Others are feeders or stepping stones to other employers. These interdependencies extend to network structures beyond individual organizations. Through them, individual workers become situated within hierarchies of organizations linked into networks, or, to be more precise, they are linked to particular positions within specific other organizations. Incomes are attached to the worker's position in these hierarchies.

If wage structures are products of interdependencies among work organizations, it is inappropriate to treat an individual's income as an independent event; yet that is precisely the assumption behind regression analysis models—models that have prevailed in the sociological studies of social stratification over the past twenty-five years. We have introduced another way to handle the kind of interdependencies mentioned. This model can be expressed mathematically, and it can account for much of the complexity involved.

More recently, many sociologists have been trying to account for income distribution from differences between industries. The results have been disappointing. In place of industry, we see compelling reasons to look instead at work organizations and occupational roles within them. There is little direct correspondence between classifications of industries and characteristics of the work organizations included in them. Any industry includes assorted work organizations, which may have different job structures that link them into different types of career networks. As a result, there will be different patterns of income transfers within a given industry.

Wages are influenced by the structure of career ladders within organizations. Career ladders have the following consequences:

1. The earnings of workers are dependent on their positions within interconnected administrative structures of large private and public bureaucracies.

2. Beyond the entry level, job ladders insulate workers from competition from outside the occupation and outside particular organizations (Sorenson and Kalleberg, 1981). They also minimize mobility from one type of organization to another, especially above the lowest levels of the career ladder.

CHAPTER 7

Structural Equivalence
and Clique Analysis

Until now, we have been concentrating on conceptual issues entangled in organizational relationships. In this and the final chapter, we shall focus more sharply on some ways to analyze the pivotal notion of interdependence. This chapter introduces the topic; however, our main message is reserved for Chapter 8, namely, that the input–output framework provides a better way to handle interdependence than other approaches being used. Its advantages will be better appreciated after considering the alternatives in this chapter.

To study networks, one must first identify their boundaries and group their members. Structural equivalence and clique analysis are two ways to group entities. *Structural equivalence* is associated with the resource dependence approach. Organizational network models are said to be sophisticated extensions of it (Pfeffer, 1982). The other alternative, *clique analysis,* is sometimes called the graph theoretic approach (Laumann and Knoke, 1987). Both approaches have advantages and disadvantages, but they are antithetical. Thus, according to structural equivalence, organizations must be grouped by how they all relate to the same actors outside the set. This method of defining a network does not consider how organizations relate to one another within the set. On the other hand, the graph theory approach (clique analysis) focuses on the reverse. It groups organizations based on how organizations within a set relate to one another, irrespective of how they relate to outside actors. Both possibilities can be accommodated with the input–output model.

It is important to remember that the following discussion is primarily concerned with the analytic techniques as they are actually being used in research, as distinguished from theoretical expositions. Several important dimensions of interorganizational relationships that theorists have mentioned, we find, either are being totally ignored in empirical studies or are not being given the priority they deserve. We suspect that the omissions are due largely to the type of analytic models being used. In the next chapter, we shall try to show how the input–output model can overcome the deficiencies of the other two popular approaches.

RESOURCE DEPENDENCE

The resource dependence approach rests on several basic assumptions. The main assumptions are these:

- Organizations are the most fundamental social unit.
- Social life takes place within networks of organizations.
- Every organization is constrained by relationships with other organizations within its network.
- Organizations try to manage these constraints, often unsuccessfully.
- Patterns of relationships engender power structures within and between the organizations involved (Pfeffer, 1982).

Discussions of the approach are usually couched in terms of information such as that contained in Table 7.1. In this table, z_{ij} stands for the dollar amounts of products sold by establishment i to establishment j (or from ith group of establishments to jth group of establishments).

According to the assumptions, constraint is the critical force in such a system. Establishment i will be constrained as other organizations make demands on it that limit its degrees of freedom. For example, a labor union in a factory obtains costly benefits, which forces prices to increase, thus undercutting the company's competitive advantage. The capacity of laborers to unite constrains the factory's ability to contain costs. Monopolists generally can charge more for their products and services because they have fewer constraints. Oil prices are usually higher if oil producers form a cartel, enabling them to control production and prices.

Basic Propositions

These general observations can be summarized as follows:

Proposition 1. If an organization obtains inputs from a single supplier, or an organized group of suppliers, it will pay more for them. On the other hand, if inputs come from competitive sources or sectors, prices will be lower.

Table 7.1
Seller–Buyer Relationships: Dollar Values of Sales

	Buyer 1	Buyer 2	...	Buyer j	...	Buyer m
Seller 1	z_{11}	z_{12}	...	z_{1j}	...	z_{1m}
Seller 2	z_{21}	z_{22}	...	z_{2j}	..	z_{2m}
...	...	...	...	...	...	
Seller m	z_{m1}	z_{m2}	...	z_{mj}	...	z_{mm}

Someone using this reasoning will come to the following prediction:

Proposition 2. The more severe the constraints on the focal organization, the more effort it will expend to build interorganizational relations aimed at reducing or avoiding their impact (Pfeffer, 1982).

Such relationships include interlocking boards, mergers, coalitions, and associations.

Reservations

The logic behind Proposition 2 eludes us. The picture we get is an organization continually responding to external threats from another, unfriendly organization. In Pfeffer's words, "[The] focal organization must attend to the demands of those in its environment that provide resources necessary and important for its continued survival" (1982: 193). The external environment is made out to be a fickle supplier of resources and a source of myriad constraints, and not much more. For protection, every organization seeks alliances with another organization. The power balance favors the environment.

We see three serious problems with this perspective: (1) it focuses exclusively on one side of a relationship; (2) it is preoccupied with dyadic relationships between a focal organization and a partner; and (3) it addresses power relationships only implicitly, not directly.

One-Sidedness. The first problem is that relationships are pictured as running in only one direction, from the environment to the focal organization. As one writer puts it, "The concept of constraint implies that one actor constrains the other. . . . Yet interindustry relations tend to be relatively symmetric" (Mizruchi, 1989: 407). In a word, the idea of interdependence requires us to consider both sides of reciprocal relationships, whereas a constraint goes one way.

This shortcoming probably is not inherent in the resource dependence perspective. The literature does portray organizational fields as systems of interaction based on exchange relationships (see, for example, Aiken and Hage, 1968; Cook and Witmeyer, 1992; Galaskiewicz and Wasserman, 1981), yet in some influential studies, environments get treated more like constraining forces than partners exchanging resources and services. For example, under a heading titled "Exchange and Dependence," Aldrich quickly switches to the notion of adaptation:

Leaders and administrators also must find ways of adapting to the pressures from organizations competing for the same resources.

He goes on to say that the resource dependence perspective is

a specification of how authorities and members behave within the constraints of their environment. (1979: 266–267)

Therefore, like the population ecology model, resource dependence stresses the dominating influence of the outside environment.

Meanings of Efficiency. Fuzziness about the two-way flow of relationships is evident in some puzzling discussions of efficiency. Some writers believe that organizations enter relationships only to minimize costs. In their view, efficiency imposes a major constraint on organizations. Not all writers would agree. In Chapter 4, we talked about the reasons organizations form relationships. Beyond the economic and political benefits they may derive, organizations associate among themselves because of laws and to satisfy mutual goals. Sometimes normative reasons, which are based on reciprocity and trust, predominate (Powell, 1990).

Putting that aside for the moment, let us follow the economic argument. We are told that pressure to be efficient comes from two sources: (1) product–market competition and (2) markets for capital and corporate control. The former, through "natural selection pressures," creates a strain toward efficiency, eliminating inefficient organizations in the process:

The forces of competition in the product market will not permit the manager to stray far from the norm of profit maximization if the firm is to remain viable. (McEachern 1975: 35)

The second type of external constraint involves the following scenario: Inefficiency leads to lowering of share prices, which, in turn, invites takeover by an outsider who can run the organization more efficiently.

The difficulty here is that the meaning of efficiency depends on what one assumes about maximizing profits. Maximization can be conditional, that is, with the prices of inputs and resources on hand fixed. Or, it can be unconditional, in which case prices and resources also will vary in ways that depend on the focal organization's ability to manipulate the environment through merger, and the like. Again, it is a question of whether one assumes a one-way relationship with the organization fixed in place or a relationship that goes both ways, allowing the organization to change its position. The conditional form is unrealistic. The unconditional form renders Proposition 2 (stated on p. 107) true by definition and, therefore, redundant and useless.

Confusion between Dependence and Constraint. Authors sometimes use the terms "dependence" and "constraint" interchangeably. One writes, "Intercorporate relations can be understood as a product of patterns of interorganizational dependence and constraint" (Pfeffer, 1987: 40). From the context, it appears he is using the terms dependence and constraint interchangeably. However, the two notions describe different aspects of an association. Constraint emphasizes one side of the relationship, namely, the ability of one organization to compel another to do, or not to do, something. Dependence refers to a contingent relationship, which is not so restrictive. Two organizations can be mutually dependent, as in an equal exchange.

Here is another instance of ambiguity. It is common sense that a constraint is a form of relationship. Therefore, what does it mean to say that "intercorporate relations will be pursued to reduce constraints on profits" (Pfeffer, 1987: 41)? We can only surmise that the intercorporate relationship referred to is a new alliance created to alter an existing relationship that hurts profits. For example, the focal organization enters a merger with a supplier to stabilize the input flow or to reduce the cost of the input. All that says is that, under certain circumstances, some relationships tend to beget other relationships. Our point is that the analytic techniques that are being extensively used with this approach do not give priority to mutual dependence, despite lip service to its importance.

Preoccupation with Dyadic Relationships. The literature on networks, which we reviewed in Chapter 4, emphasizes that network partners must engage in indirect relationships. It is widely acknowledged, for example, that ties in networks are transitive. In other words, direct ties between *A* and *B,* and between *B* and *C,* imply an indirect link between *A* and *C*. Indirect partners are useful when direct ties are difficult to maintain, as happens when two co-workers, for example, feud among themselves and rely on a mutual associate to relay messages between them (Wellman, 1988: 42). The import of indirect links among network members is Wellman's second principle of structural analysis (p. 41).

Nevertheless, the conventional techniques only account for direct relationships between two (or possibly a few) organizations (see, for example, Larson, 1992). Because feedback from indirect partners seldom has been examined, the inherent complexities have been glossed over. For example, Galaskiewicz and Wasserman (1981) used a discrete-time version of Marcok chains to analyze the degree of reciprocity among corporations in the way they assign members to their boards. That study does meet our first objection in that it is concerned with reciprocal relationships; however, it considers only dyadic relationships. Burt (1983) proposed the following index of external constraint imposed by establishments in industry i on the establishments in industry j:

$$[(\text{sales to } i/\text{total sales})^2 + (\text{purchases from } i/\text{total purchases})^2] \, y_i$$

The term y_i is a measure of the imperfect competition among establishments in industry i. One could measure it, for example, by the four-firm concentration ratio.[1] These discrete measures of competition can be aggregated over all industries in the economy to obtain a general measure of external constraint on the establishments in industry j (Burt, 1983: 39).

According to this approach, an organization's dependence on entity E can be expressed as a function of two measures:

1. the proportion of transactions with that entity;
2. the degree to which E is a monopoly.

This idea has been in the literature for some time (Pfeffer and Salancik, 1978). Burt (1983) is credited with showing specifically how to predict where constraints are likely to be greatest and when efforts will be made to manage them. He used an input–output table for the economy (see, for example, Pfeffer, 1987: 42).[2]

The Significance of Feedback. Looking at dependence and constraints as *dyadic* transactions, as Burt advocates, has a distinct disadvantage. It fails to recognize that sales and purchases can have direct and indirect feedback effects. For example, suppose a firm manufactures commercial aircraft, and it has a subsidiary that manufactures extruded aluminum shapes. Suppose also that this firm buys jet engines from another firm that specializes in manufacturing them. Now, an increase in demand for aircraft manufactured by the firm in question increases the demand for jet engines. In turn, it increases the demand for all the direct and indirect inputs for the manufacture of jet engines, one of which might be extruded aluminum shapes. We have here a direct feedback effect.

In addition, there are indirect feedbacks, operating through intermediaries: *A* needs *C*'s output to produce something *B* needs. If *C* does not provide it, *B* will be affected, although *B* does not interact directly with *C*. Such feedbacks cannot be fully captured if attention is confined to a dyadic seller–buyer relationship. An organization can be in the environment of another even if the relationship between them is only indirect.

Neglect of Power. The third shortcoming inherent in the analytic models being used is the tendency to treat power relationships in an implicit way. It is generally acknowledged that power is a product of dependency relationships (Cook and Emerson, 1984; Emerson, 1962: 33). Party *A* in a relationship has power to the extent that the other party *(B)* is dependent on *A*. Furthermore, dependence is decided by the importance *B* places on goals mediated by *A* and by *B*'s ability to obtain these goals from other sources. Yet while power structures are mentioned in theoretical discussions of resource dependence, systematic attempts to link power structures empirically to the seller–buyer matrix shown in Table 7.1 are scarce. In Chapter 8, we will show that the input–output approach provides a systematic way to handle direct and indirect relationships, and direct and indirect feedbacks, which are so clearly implied in a matrix of interdependencies. These relationships are central to power defined as a matrix of dependencies.

To provide a background for our discussion of the input–output framework in the final chapter, we comment briefly on structural equivalence and other related ideas commonly used in the study of organizational interdependence. To study an organizational network, one has to identify its boundaries and be prepared to explain how its members exercise influence over one another. Two approaches have been used. One is to map the direct and indirect contacts among member organizations; organizations without ties are not part of the network. The other approach is to identify role sets comprising similar organizations whose only connections may be through symbolically shared norms. The first approach identifies *cliques*. Clique relations take many forms, such as: (a) an officer in one corporation is also a member of another organization's board of directors; (b) manufacturing firms, which have a common interest in reducing trade restrictions, organize to lobby for legislation. The second approach requires the analyst to categorize organizations according to their *structural equivalence*.

STRUCTURAL EQUIVALENCE

To be structurally equivalent, organizations must share a common locus in a social system. Organizations are structurally equivalent when they have the same relationship to each third party. For example, firms

that borrow money from the same bank(s) are, in that respect, structurally related to each other as borrowers.

Types of Equivalence

Equivalence is central to the resource dependence approach, and,
therefore, it will be useful to discuss it in more detail. Equivalence can
take at least three forms: strict, weak, and regular.

Structural Equivalence (Strict Form). Two establishments are said
to be structurally equivalent in the strict sense if, and only if, they are
identical in their relationships with other establishments in the economy. The relationships we shall be considering in this context involve
either a sale of an output or a purchase of an input (expressed in dollar
terms). Look now at the entries in Table 7.1. For establishments i and
j, the strict criterion of structural equivalence is that the zs must be
the same in rows (i and j) and in columns (i and j).

Structural Equivalence (Weak Form). Note that the above criterion
is too stringent for practical applications. A weak criterion has been
suggested in the literature. Define the term d_{ij} as follows:

$$d_{ij} = \sqrt{[\Sigma (z_{iq} - z_{jq})^2 + \Sigma (z_{qi} - z_{qj})^2]}$$

The weak criterion for structural equivalence requires only that d_{ij} is
smaller than a prespecified small quantity.[3] Note that the expression
within the radical sign has two terms. The first one is the sum of squares
of differences in zs within the rows for sellers i and j (in Table 7.1); this
excludes entries in columns i and j (i.e., z_{ii}, z_{ij}, z_{ji}, and z_{jj}). The second
term is the sum of squares for differences in zs listed in the columns for
buyers i and j (excluding entries in rows i and j).

Role Sets. Note that in this model, structurally equivalent actors occupy a position or status. The pattern of their relations with occupants
of other positions (statuses) forms the "role set" associated with their
position (Burt, 1983: 61).

In social network analysis, z_{ij} represents the value of a relation from
the ith actor directed to the jth actor (Knoke and Kuklinski, 1982: 43).
In the simplest case, each z_{ij} is either 0 or 1 (the former representing,
for example, the absence of a relationship, and the latter its presence).
The "social distance" between actors i and j is d_{ij}, as defined above. The
set of d_{ij}s is often subjected to a hierarchical cluster analysis to identify
distinct positions.

Cluster Identification. Clusters are identied in various ways. One
method starts by arranging each actor to separate positions, and then
aggregating the positions into clusters. To be placed in the same posi-

tion, two actors must have d_{ij} less than or equal to an arbitrarily chosen value, for example, α. When values of α are small, there will be many clusters; and when the values are large, there will be fewer clusters. As α progressively increases, the number of clusters diminishes until eventually all actors end in a single cluster. In practice, the analyst stops at an intermediate stage by setting the α on substantive grounds, that is, by using a reasonable weak criterion.

Block Modeling. Block modeling is another approach that has been used frequently to group actors into structurally equivalent positions (blocks). In this approach, all actors are put in one cluster, which is then progressively subdivided. A widely used block-modeling algorithm is CONCOR (CONvergence of iterated CORrelations). The CONCOR is a hierarchical clustering procedure that partitions a set of actors into progressively larger blocks of actors. It starts with a set of matrixes, each representing a network of relations among a given set of actors.

For example, the starting relationships may be international trade flows involving two specific commodities (e.g., raw materials, machinery). The matrixes are stacked, one below the other. If there are k matrixes and n actors, the stacked matrix has n columns and $k \times n$ rows. CONCOR calculates product–moment correlations between each pair of columns of this stacked matrix. These correlations are arranged in an n-by-n matrix. Its elements represent linear measures of similarity between each pair of actors as they relate to other actors.

The correlation matrix just described forms the basis for partitioning the actors into two blocks. After partitioning, all actors in either block are more like those in that block than like any actor in the other. The process is then repeated for each block until the analyst decides to stop. This decision must be made on substantive grounds.

Snyder and Kick (1979) applied the block-modeling technique to several types of international ties: trade, military intervention, treaty membership, and diplomatic exchanges. Using these ties, they identified ten blocks of nations. This classification was then used as a categorical (dummy-coded) independent variable in a comparative analysis of economic growth over a 15-year period. Breiger (1981) investigated trade ties among twenty-four countries belonging to the group of "core" nations that were identified in the Snyder/Kick study. He found that the so-called core was not actually homogeneous because they were differentiated with respect to economic strength and were attached to two different influence centers: either Anglo-American–Japanese or European.

Smith and White (1992) also used trade ties to partition nations into blocks. They used still another clustering algorithm called REGE, which we will not go into here. We only wanted to show that several kinds of block modeling and other approaches are available.

Implications. Reflecting on the approach mentioned above, Laumann and Knoke point out that

The structural equivalence approach thus argues for data reduction by aggregating those organizations that maintain identical or highly similar direct ties with all other domain organizations. Organizations placed together as structurally equivalent need not, however, be in direct contact with one another under this criterion. (1987: 218)

Their comment underscores a critical characteristic of the structural equivalence approach: it is *extroversive*. In other words, it looks outside the position to establish whether the position members are equivalent. Relationships within the position are immaterial.

Regular Equivalence. Smith and White maintain that structural equivalence standards are too narrow to define networks of nations. They call instead for a broader criterion. Regular equivalence, as they refer to it, is based on the following notion:

To be "regularly equivalent," two actors A and B need not have highly similar relationships with every actor in their environment. It is enough that they have similar relationships to "substitutable" actors. (1992: 860)

Two countries are equivalent if their trade relations with substitutable trade partners are equivalent. For example, assume countries X and Y trade, respectively, with z_1 and z_2. Then X and Y are regularly equivalent to the extent z_1 and z_2 have similar characteristics. Or, consider two storekeepers, C and D, who have employees E and F, respectively. C and D are regularly equivalent; E and F also are regularly equivalent. Note that structural equivalence places these four actors (i.e., E, F, C, and D) in four different positions. Smith and White claim that the regular equivalence approach "precisely identifies the more generic structural positions in a network" (1992: 860).

Notice that both approaches, regular and structural, emphasize direct relations. Also, neither approach gives any attention to direct relationships between the entities that are regarded as equivalent.

CLIQUES

A *clique* is a highly cohesive subset of actors within a network. Under the most stringent definition, a clique of organizations is a maximal subset of organizations that are all directly linked to each other. Thus defined, one clique cannot be a part of another clique. When the direction of a relationship is of interest, then in a clique consisting of three actors (A, B, and C), there are six relationships:

1. $A \rightarrow B$,
2. $A \rightarrow C$,
3. $B \rightarrow A$,
4. $B \rightarrow C$,
5. $C \rightarrow A$,
6. $C \rightarrow B$.

However, this stringent criterion is too impractical for most purposes. Some writers suggest relaxing it in various ways. According to one suggestion, a subset of organizations forms a clique if the members of that subset are directly or indirectly linked to each other—if no indirect linkage involves more than a few intermediaries.

Cliques Distinguished from Structural Equivalent Aggregates

Cliquing is an *introversive* approach; that is, to decide whether a collectivity is a clique, one must look inside it for signs of cohesiveness. A set of actors forms a clique, only if each actor is linked to each other within the set, irrespective of relationships with actors outside the set. In contrast, recall that the structural equivalence approach is *extroversive*. In other words, to decide whether the group members are structurally equivalent, one looks outside the group for similarity of ties to other domain actors. A set of actors is *structurally equivalent* if actors have the same (or virtually similar) relations with actors outside the set, regardless of their relationships within the set.

Laumann and Knoke believe actors who are structurally equivalent will have more similarities than clique members (1987: 219). We disagree. Cliques can have members who also are structurally equivalent and, therefore, share both types of similarities. The empirical question is this: What proportion of cliques also meet the criterion of structural equivalence?

Graph Theory

Clique detection is sometimes called graph theoretic aggregation. As Laumann and Knoke explain:

The graph theoretic approach argues for a data-reduction strategy that aggregates those organizations which maintain the largest number of short-distance . . . links to domain participants.[4] (1987: 218)

Burt (1983) has argued that graph theoretic aggregation (clique) is a special case of aggregation according to structural equivalence. Others disagree.

OTHER METHODS OF AGGREGATION

Researchers have used approaches other than equivalence and cliques to aggregate organizations. Dozens of typologies have been proposed (see Corwin, 1987). For example, as we noted in Chapter 5, a distinction between firms in core and periphery segments of the economy has been popular. The two types of firms are distinguished by "organizational goals and strategies, procedures for structuring work, and definitions of economic, political, and normative boundaries" (Baron and Bielby, 1984: 456). Hannan and Freeman (1984) suggested classifying organizations using their stated goals, forms of authority, core technology, and marketing strategy. In addition, one could include division of labor, standardization, or openness of boundaries. For some purposes, geographic units such as communities and regions can be used to classify organizations.

One problem that every investigator must resolve is how to identify the boundaries of nested organizational units. For example, big organizations may own subsidiaries or control international franchises. Local and branch offices of multinational corporations may have distinctive relationships with the main offices, depending on the nation's circumstances. Large automobile companies operate plants in several states in the United States. To help clarify boundary issues that can arise from such arrangements, Berkowitz has proposed a threefold typology. A *firm* is a legal entity consisting of capital and other assets held in a common name and operating plants in varied locations. The actual production units, which employ workers, are called *establishments*. Sets of firms that operate under common control and which are responsible for coordination are called *enterprises* (1988: 264–269).

CONCLUSIONS

In this chapter, some techniques for analyzing the pivotal notion of interdependence were described. We concentrated on two alternatives: structural equivalence and clique analysis. Three forms of equivalence were discussed: strict, weak, and regular. The main differences between structural equivalence and clique analysis can be summarized using a two-way table, the rows and columns of which represent categories of organizations. If there are only two categories, the arrangement has the following form:

	Class 1	Class 2
Class 1	A	B
Class 2	C	D

The structural equivalence approach is concerned with the relationship in the top-right and bottom-left cells (cells B and C). Most other approaches, except cliquing and the graph theoretic aggregation, are likely to do the same. However, clique analysis directs attention to the relationship in the top-left and bottom-right cells (cells A and D). It is our position that all four cells deserve attention.

The structural equivalence approach is closely associated with the resource dependence theory of organization–environment relationships, which treats constraint as the critical force operating on organizations. Like population ecology, resource dependence stresses the dominating influence of the outside environment. Every organization is portrayed as continually responding to external threats from another, unfriendly organization.

We noted three problems with this perspective. First, it suggests that relationships only go one way. The analytic techniques being used extensively with this approach do not give priority to mutual dependence, notwithstanding the lip service often paid to its importance. Second, it is preoccupied with dyadic relationships between a focal organization and a partner. Some authors treat dependence and constraint as dyadic transactions. This approach fails to recognize that sales and purchases can have direct and indirect feedback effects. Because investigators seldom examine the feedback from indirect partners, the inherent complexities have been glossed over. Third, it slights the implicit power relationships. While power structures are often mentioned in theoretical discussions of resource dependence, it is hard to find systematic attempts to link power structures empirically to the seller–buyer relationships.

The input–output framework, the subject of the following chapter, overcomes many of these problems.

NOTES

1. Let s_1 be the largest market share of any corporation within an industry, s_2 the next largest market share, and so on. $C_{14} = s_1 + s_2 + s_3 + s_4$, which is the sum of the four largest market shares of corporations within an industry, is the four-firm concentration ratio.

2. Burt (1983) advanced the thesis that American economy operates simultaneously as a competitive market and a managed market. Competitive forces created in the network of buying and selling constrain corporate profits. The

social network of directorate ties lessen the impact of these constraints on profits.

3. A minimum size (e.g., of three actors) is also commonly prescribed (Cartwright and Harary, 1956).

4. Distance is measured by path. To define *path*, it is convenient to think of a road map as a graph (i.e., points joined by lines). If v_i are labels for points in a graph, a finite sequence of the form $v_0 \rightarrow v_1 \rightarrow \ldots \rightarrow v_m$ is called a *walk*, in which $v_0 \rightarrow v_1$, etc., are lines; a walk in which all the lines are distinct is called a *trail*; a trail in which all points (v_0, v_1, etc.) are also distinct (except, possibly, $v_0 = v_m$) is a *path*. If each line of a graph has a weight of one, then the shortest path from one point, *A*, to another, *B*, is the smallest number of lines needed to go from *A* to *B*.

CHAPTER 8

The Input–Output Framework

Several investigations have been concerned with how resources flow through networks (Galaskiewicz and Marsden, 1989). However, as we have said, most of the studies to date have used models that omit important dimensions of the process. We believe that the input–output model corrects some of these deficiencies. Aldrich reports that Pennings (in an unpublished paper) borrowed Leontief's model of input–output analyses of interindustry transactions (1979: 282). Such a model can be used to show that relations between buyers and sellers in a given market can be understood as a matrix of resource–exchange transactions. In principle, any organizational network can be represented as a matrix. The input–output model relies on matrix analysis. Basic expositions can be found in Richardson (1972) and Miller and Blair (1985), among others.

THE TRADITIONAL INPUT–OUTPUT TABLE

A traditional input–output table is constructed from observed data for a given area, such as a nation or region. We begin with sets of organizations representing industries within a nation and then turn to regions. Assume that economic activity is divided into several segments or producing sectors. These may be organizations within industries or aggregations of them. When we use the term "industry" in the following discussion, it should be understood as a shorthand label for all organizations making up the industry. In practice, of course, complete populations of organizations often must be represented by stratified samples. The essential data are the flows of products from each sector (as a producer) to each sector (as a purchaser). These flows are measured for a particular period (e.g., one year) and in monetary terms (e.g., dollar values).

Table 8.1
Seller–Buyer Relationships: Dollar Values of Items Sold

	Buyer 1	Buyer 2	...	Buyer j	...	Buyer m
Seller 1	z_{11}	z_{12}	...	z_{1j}	...	z_{1m}
Seller 2	z_{21}	z_{22}	...	z_{2j}	...	z_{2m}
...	...	...	...	...	...	
Seller m	z_{m1}	z_{m2}	...	z_{mj}	...	z_{mm}

Basic Concepts: Interindustry Flows

Denote the observed monetary value of the flow from producing organizations comprising industry i to producing organizations in industry j by z_{ij}. Then the interindustry flows among producing organizations can be displayed in summary form, as in Table 8.1. Beyond the interindustry flows, there are flows to purchasers who are more external to the industrial sectors of the economy. Households, government, and foreign buyers are obvious examples. There is a major distinction between such buyers and producing organizations themselves. When industries use products, it is for the purpose of manufacturing still other products that consumers can use. The other types of buyers, on the other hand, consume the products. Therefore, the flows to the buyers external to the industrial sectors are called *final demand*.

Other Basic Concepts

Other ideas basic to the input–output framework can be illustrated with a simple numerical example (Table 8.2). For the moment, the components of final demand (i.e., households, governments, foreign buyers, etc.) are not distinguished. Also, the components of inputs other than industrial products are all lumped together. In addition, the different types of organizations comprising an industry are aggregated and simply called an industry. Finally, for simplicity it is assumed that each industry produces a single commodity. In research, of course, it is essential to disaggregate these dimensions.

Producers in Industry 1 produce an output worth $100. Of this, 15 percent is consumed by producing organizations within the industry itself, 50 percent is sold to Industry 2, and the remaining 35 percent goes to final demand. Industry 2 produces a commodity worth $200. It consumes 5 percent of this output, 10 percent is sold to Industry 1,

Table 8.2
A Hypothetical Input–Output Transaction Table

	Industry 1	Industry 2	Final Demand	Total Output
Sellers				
Industry 1	15	50	35	100
Industry 2	20	10	170	200
Other sources	65	140	110	315
Total outlays	100	200	315	615

and 85 percent goes to final demand. The third row shows goods and services sold by other sellers outside the industrial sector, including labor, entrepreneurial services, capital, and the like.

Note that the row sums are the same as the column sums. Reading down a column, one finds inputs. Thus, to produce $200 worth of its output, organizations comprising Industry 2 use $50 worth of products produced by organizations in Industry 1, $10 worth of products from Industry 2, and $140 worth of products from other sellers. Expressed in per dollar terms, these inputs give the so-called input coefficients: a_{12} = 50/200 and a_{22} = 10/200. The corresponding input coefficients for Industry 1 are a_{11} = 15/100 and a_{21} = 20/100.

Thus, to produce a dollar worth of Industry 1's output, the needed inputs are:

$0.15 worth of Industry 1's product,

$0.20 worth of Industry 2's product, and

$0.65 worth of other goods and services.

These numbers, written as an array, form the vector (0.15 0.20 0.65), which is the ingredient makeup of Industry 1's product. The corresponding ingredient makeup of Industry 2's product is (0.25 0.05 0.70). Note that the elements of these arrays have unity for their sum. Therefore, if we know the first two, which are the industrial components in the array, we know the rest (i.e., the nonindustrial component).

Predicting Equations. It is commonly assumed that the input coefficients (the industrial components of the arrays mentioned above) remain the same, irrespective of the volume of output. It is further assumed that these are time-invariant, at least in the short run. The latter assumption implies that the technology of production (ingredient composition of products) remains fixed. Under these assumptions, we can generalize the following flow equation for Industry 1

$$0.15 \times 100 + 0.25 \times 200 + 35 = 100$$

to this:

$$0.15x_1 + 0.25x_2 + f_1 = x_1 \tag{1}$$

In this latter equation, x_1 and x_2 are the volumes of outputs of Industries 1 and 2, respectively; f_1 is the final demand for Industry 1. Similarly, for Industry 2 we have:

$$20x_1 + 0.05x_2 + f_2 = x_2 \tag{2}$$

Given f_1 and f_2, then from equations (1) and (2), it is clear that we can predict x_1 and x_2. The predicting equations are:

$$x_1 = (380/303)f_1 + (100/303)f_2 \tag{3}$$

$$x_2 = (80/303)f_1 + (340/303)f_2 \tag{4}$$

These equations imply the following equations relating change in gross output to changes in the final demand:

$$\text{Change in } x_1 = (380/303)\,\Delta f_1 + (100/303)\,\Delta f_2 \tag{5}$$

$$\text{Change in } x_2 = (80/303)\,\Delta f_1 + (340/303)\,\Delta f_2 \tag{6}$$

Power. If f_2 remains unchanged, then a change in f_1 equal to Δf_1 generates a change in x_1 of magnitude: $(380/303) \times \Delta f_1$ (i.e., $1.254 \times \Delta f_1$). In x_2, the change is: $(80/303) \times \Delta f_1$ (i.e., $0.264 \times \Delta f_1$). If we say that $\Delta f_1 = \$1.00$, it means that the dollar value of changing final demand for the product of Industry 1 is $1.00. The effect of that change on Industry 1's gross output (in dollar value) is $1.254. This represents $1.00 to satisfy the increase in the final demand as such and an additional

$0.254 used exclusively by Industries 1 and 2. This latter component stems from the interdependence of the two industries (see the comments on feedback relations given earlier).

The corresponding effect on x_2 is $0.264 \times \Delta f_1$, which is for exclusive intra- and interindustry use. The total effect divided by Δf_1 is a dimensionless number:

$$[1.254 \, (\Delta f_1) + 0.264 \, (\Delta f_1)]/\Delta f_1 = 1.518$$

This number is called the output multiplier for Industry 1. Notice that this is the sum of the coefficients of f_1 in equations (3) and (4). The corresponding output multiplier for Industry 2 is 1.452, which is the sum of the coefficients of f_2 in equations (3) and (4).

Therefore, in this economy, an additional dollar would yield maximum impact if it is spent in Industry 1. Similarly, any reduction in investment in Industry 1 would affect the economy more than a corresponding reduction of investment in Industry 2. In this sense, we may say that Industry 1 has more power than Industry 2.

The Leontief Inverse. The coefficients of f_1 and f_2 in equations (3) and (4) thus reflect crucial features of the interdependence of the industries 1 and 2 and their relationships with the environment. These coefficients are arranged below in a row-by-column format, call it matrix B:

Matrix B

$$\begin{pmatrix} 380/303 & 100/303 \\ 80/303 & 340/303 \end{pmatrix}$$

This matrix is related to the corresponding matrix (matrix A) of input coefficients:

Matrix A

$$\begin{pmatrix} .15 & .25 \\ .20 & .05 \end{pmatrix}$$

in the following fashion,

$$B = \text{Inverse of } (I - A).$$

As a rule, if A is the matrix of input coefficients, then the inverse of $(I - A)$ is called the *Leontief inverse* of A. It can be shown that

$$\text{the Leontief inverse of } A = I + A + A^2 + A^3 + \ldots \quad (6)$$

I is the identity matrix having the same number of rows (columns) as A.

Direct and Indirect Effects

In the discussion of multipliers, the term I on the right-hand side of equation (6) is regarded by some writers as the "initial effect." A is the "direct effect," and the $(A^2 + A^3 + \ldots)$ the "indirect effect." This term is to be understood in the following sense. Consider a simple economy with two industries. Suppose its 2-by-2 input coefficient matrix is as given above, with 0.15 and 0.25 as the first row and 0.20 and 0.05 as the second row. Suppose an exogenously generated final demand is for $60 worth of products of Industry 1 and $150 worth of products of Industry 2. Now consider the components of the response of the industries to this new final demand.

1. Clearly, each industry must produce at least as much as the new final demand: Industry 1 needs to produce at least $60 worth of its output, and Industry 2 needs to produce at least $150 worth of its output. This is not all, though.

2. To produce $60 worth of its output, Industry 1 needs, as inputs, $9 worth (0.15 × $60) of its own products and $12 worth (0.20 × $60) of products from Industry 2. Note that 0.15 and 0.20 are from column 1 of the matrix of input coefficients.

3. Similarly, to produce $150 worth of its output, Industry 2 needs, as inputs, $37.5 worth (0.25 × $150) of Industry 1's products. It also needs $7.5 worth (0.05 × $150) of its own products.

4. What this all means is that Industry 1 must produce $60 worth of its products [as mentioned in (1) above] plus $46.5 more (i.e., $9 + $37.5) to meet input needs. Similarly, Industry 2's output must be at least $150 plus $19.5 more (i.e., $12 + $7.5).

The flows attributable to input needs mentioned in (2) above are $46.5 and $19.5 from Industries 1 and 2. These two flows, in turn, require still other interindustry flows. They, in turn, generate additional flows, and so on. The additions become progressively smaller at each round, and after several rounds, they become negligible. This can be illustrated as follows:

Round	1	2	3	4	5	6	7	
Industry 1	$46.5	11.85	4.35	1.37	0.46	0.15	0.05	...
Industry 2	$19.5	10.28	2.88	1.01	0.33	0.01	0.04	...

Notice that if f stands for the new final demand expressed as a column vector, then the product Af gives the first-round additions. The product

A^2f gives the second-round additions, and so on. Thus, $(A + A^2 + A^3 + ...)f$ gives the sum of all the additions, that is, the sum of the direct and indirect impacts of the final demand. These features display the importance of the elements of the Leontief inverse.

We believe that the interdependence of industries can be best represented by the elements of the Leontief inverse because they capture the direct and indirect responses to changes in the final demand. A logical method of grouping industries, if they must be grouped, is in terms of the distance between their respective columns in the Leontief inverse.

Another Look at Structural Equivalence

The distance measures commonly used in the structural equivalence approach to partition industries into positions are based on output flows and, therefore, fail to capture interdependence as we defined it above. To appreciate this point, recall that the distance measure used in question is the following:

$$d_{ij} = \sqrt{[\Sigma (z_{iq} - z_{jq})^2 + \Sigma (z_{qi} - z_{qj})^2]}$$

where zs are the flows that are shown in the example of Table 8.1. This measure, d_{ij}, has the potential for being unstable over time, and it is likely to be sensitive to small fluctuations in observations (zs). Furthermore, it cannot be interpreted in terms of direct and indirect responses to final demand changes. The last is true also of a distance measure that was used by Blin and Cohen (1977). Their measure used (direct) input coefficients, specifically expressed as the sum of squares for differences of columns for A:

$$d_{ij} = \sqrt{[\Sigma (a_{qi} - b_{qj})^2]}$$

The logic underlying any particular clustering procedure one may choose to adopt is not a matter of indifference. This is especially true if in subsequent analyses each cluster is used as an undifferentiated aggregate and if relationships among the actors within the aggregate (cluster) are ignored. That is usually the case. If, however, the relationships within the cluster are duly included in one's analyses, the particular algorithm used for clustering may not matter very much for most practical purposes.

The Concept of Constraint Revisited

We are now ready to offer an alternative to the resource dependency approach to so-called "external" constraint. According to the resource-dependency perspective, the external constraint on group j that is exerted by group i is calculated as the product of

$$[(\text{sales to group } i/\text{total sales})^2 + (\text{purchases from group } i/\text{total purchases})^2] \, y_i$$

with y_i (e.g., the four-firm concentration ratio) as a measure of imperfect competition of group i. Obviously, this way of assessing constraint does not capture fully all relationships among the industry groups involved. A more defensible way of representing constraint is via the columns of the Leontief inverse − I because this quantity, as was pointed out, captures the direct and indirect constraints.

COMMODITY-BY-INDUSTRY MODELS

Thus far, attention has been confined to the traditional input–output model. Next, we turn to some modern developments in dealing with input–output relationships. As mentioned earlier, the data for most modern input–output tables are obtained through censuses (or surveys) of industrial firms located within a region or nation of interest. In compiling the data, firms are grouped according to a standardized classification scheme. For example, in the United States, a classification has been prepared by the U.S. Department of Commerce for this purpose. It is called the Standard Industrial Classification (SIC).

In census and surveys, information collected from individual establishments (where industrial operations are performed) includes the following:

• inputs, outputs, employee compensation, profit-type income;
• capital consumption allowances, indirect business taxes, imports, exports, government purchases of goods and services; and
• sales to households (for personal consumption).

Data must be collected from firms belonging to each Standard Industrial Class and then aggregated.

The Anomaly of Secondary Products

A firm is assigned to a Standard Industrial Class solely because of its primary product. It might produce a secondary product besides the primary one, but that does not matter. The entire value of the output of both products is assigned to the classification dictated by the primary product. This yields misleading pictures when the secondary production is significant (Griffin, 1976).

Table 8.3
Basic Structure of a Commodity-by-Industry Compilation

	Commodities A B . . .	Industries A B . .	Final Demand	Total Output
Commodities A B . . .		U	E (Column)	Q
Industries A B . .	V			
Value Added*		W (Row)	**	
Total Inputs				

*Employee compensation (payment for labor services), taxes paid (for government services), profit (payment for entrepreneurship), interest (payment for capital), rental payments, and so on. Since column sums should equal the row sums, certain components of value added are sometimes obtained by subtraction.
**The column sum of E is equal to row sum of W.

The problem could be avoided if it were possible to collect all necessary information separately for every commodity a firm produces. However, these details ordinarily are not available. Perhaps a firm producing both assembled automobiles and parts does not routinely record inputs used for each commodity separately.

The Commodity-by-Industry Table

One method that has been developed to cope with this problem is the so-called commodity-by-industry table. Table 8.3 shows the basic structure of a commodity-by-industry compilation of input–output data.

The symbols used in Table 8.3 are defined as follows:

V is called the make matrix; it has n rows and m columns. The entry in the ij cell is the amount of commodity j that industry i produces.

U is called the use matrix; it has m rows and n columns. Its ij entry is the amount of commodity i that industry j uses.

Table 8.4
A Numerical Example of a Commodity-by-Industry Account

	Commodities A B	Industries A B	Final Demand	Total Output
Commodities A B		10 10 U 10 4	80 E 86	100 Q 100
Industries A B	85 0 V 15 100			85 X 115
Value Added		65 101 W	166	
Total Outputs	100 100	85 115		(200)

E is a column vector with m entries. Its ith entry is the total volume (or value of it in monetary units) of commodity i delivered to final demand.

Q is a column vector with m entries. Its ith entry is the gross output of commodity i.

W is a row vector of value-added inputs. It has n entries. Its ith entry refers to industry i.

X is a column vector of gross outputs. It has n entries. Its ith entry refers to industry i.

Most of the time, the number of distinct commodities is equal to the number of industries. This is because each commodity is treated as the primary product of at least one firm. However, the number of industries can be symbolized by n, and m can be used for the number of distinct commodities. A numerical example (using hypothetical figures) is given in Table 8.4, with two industries and two commodities.

In Table 8.4, $n = m = 2$. Notice that the sum of the entries in the ith row of V equal the ith entry of X. In Table 8.4, $85 + 0 = 85$; $15 + 100 = 115$. In general (Table 8.3):

$$V_{i1} + V_{i2} + \ldots + V_{im} = X_i \qquad (7)$$

This equation says that the total output of an industry is equal to the sum of the values of commodities produced by that industry.

Commodity Balance Equation. Also notice that the sum of the entries in the ith row of U plus the corresponding entry of E is equal to the ith entry of Q. In Table 8.4, $10 + 10 + 80 = 100$; $10 + 4 + 86 = 100$. In general (Table 8.3):

$$u_{i1} + u_{i2} + \ldots + u_{in} + E_i = Q_i \tag{8}$$

This is called the *commodity balance equation*. It simply says that the total production of a commodity is equal to the sum of the amounts of that commodity consumed by industries (in their respective production processes) plus any sales of that commodity to final consumers. Let us define b_{ij}s as

$$b_{i1} = u_{i1}/X_1, \; b_{i2} = u_{i2}/X_2, \ldots, \; b_{in} = u_{in}/X_n \tag{9}$$

Basic Identities. The above equations contain properties that are analogous to the basic identities in the traditional Leontief model. For example, in Table 8.4,

$$b_{11} = 10/85; \; b_{12} = 10/115$$
$$b_{21} = 10/85; \; b_{22} = 4/115$$

In equation (8), it is possible to substitute $b_{i1}X_1$ for u_{i1}, and $b_{i2}X_2$ for u_{i2}, and so on. After these substitutions, we have:

$$b_{i1}X_1 + b_{i2}X_2 + \ldots + b_{in}X_n + E_i = Q_i \tag{10}$$

This equation is analogous to the basic identity in the traditional Leontief model. It says that the total industry output is equal to deliveries to industries for intermediate production plus deliveries to final demand.

Another basic identity is that the sum of all commodity inputs plus value-added inputs is equal to the value of that commodity's total output. In Table 8.4, $10 + 10 + 65 = 85$; $10 + 4 + 101 = 115$. In general (Table 8.3):

$$u_{1j} + u_{2j} + \ldots + u_{mj} + W_j = X_j \tag{11}$$

Industry-by-Industry Requirement Matrix

Now recall that the ij element of the Leontief inverse in the traditional input–output model represents the output of industry i that is directly or indirectly required to deliver one dollar's worth of industry j's product to final demand. Therefore, the Leontief inverse may be called an "industry-by-industry requirement matrix" to phrase it in terms of the traditional input–output model. We have already seen the importance of this matrix for capturing interdependence among industries, showing relative power of an industry, and the like. In the commodity-by-industry model, we can have several such total requirements matrixes, including one for the commodity-by-commodity matrix and one for the industry-by-commodity matrix.

Industry-Based Technology Assumptions. Let us denote by d_{ij} industry i's output of commodity j as a fraction of the total amount of that commodity in the economy:

$$d_{ij} = v_{ij}/Q_j \tag{12}$$

Thus defined d_{ij}s are the industry-specific commodity output proportions (not to be confused with the distance measures mentioned earlier, concerning the discussion of structural equivalence). In Table 8.4,

$$d_{11} = 85/100 = 0.85 \quad d_{12} = 0/100 = 0$$
$$d_{21} = 15/100 = 0.15 \quad d_{22} = 100/100 = 1$$

We assume that d_{ij} remains the same, irrespective of the size of Q_j (the commodity output). We further assume that d_{ij} remains time-invariant, at least in the short run. These assumptions parallel those we made earlier with respect to a_{ij}s related to the traditional input–output model.

These assumptions about d_{ij}s make up what is often called *industry-based technology assumptions*. They say that the input structure of an industry is independent of its output product mix. In other words, the same input structure is used for each commodity that an industry produces. Alternatively, one could use the *commodity-based technology assumptions*. They say that a commodity has the same input structure no matter which industry produces it. (See, for example, Miller and Blair, 1985: 169–174.)

Now imagine that d_{ij}s have been calculated from data collected in one year. Assume also that the same information applies to subsequent years. If v_{ij} and Q_j are treated as unspecified quantities, from equation (12) and for a given d_{ij} we have

$$v_{ij} = d_{ij}Q_j \tag{13}$$

In the particular illustrative case under consideration,

$$v_{11} = d_{11}Q_1 = 0.85Q_1 \quad v_{12} = d_{12}Q_2 = 0 \tag{14}$$
$$v_{21} = d_{21}Q_1 = 0.15Q_1 \quad v_{22} = d_{22}Q_2 = Q_2$$

Recall that the sum of the entries in row i of the matrix V is equal to X_i. Therefore, from equation (7) we have

$$0.85Q_1 = X_1 \qquad (15)$$
$$0.15Q_1 + Q_2 = X_2$$

Now notice that equation (10) becomes the following in the particular illustrative case at hand:

$$b_{11}X_1 + b_{12}X_2 + E_1 = Q_1$$
$$b_{21}X_1 + b_{22}X_2 + E_2 = Q_2$$

Or, after inserting the calculated values of b_{ij}s computed earlier,

$$(10/85)X_1 + (10/115)X_2 + E_1 = Q_1 \qquad (16)$$
$$(10/85)X_1 + (4/115)X_2 + E_2 = Q_2$$

Next, substitute in these equations the expressions for X_is from equation (15). After simplification, this gives

$$0.1Q_1 + (0.6/115)Q_1 + (4/115)Q_2 + E_1 = Q_1$$
$$-0.1Q_1 + (1.5/115)Q_2 + (10/115)Q_2 + E_2 = Q_2$$

Bringing the terms expressed in Qs to one side, we obtain

$$(102/115)Q_1 - (10/115)Q_2 = E_1 \qquad (17)$$
$$-(12.1/115)Q_1 + (111/115)Q_2 = E_2$$

From this, when Qs are expressed in terms of Es, we obtain

$$1.13963E_1 + 0.10267E_2 = Q_1 \qquad (18)$$
$$0.12423E_1 + 1.04723E_2 = Q_2$$

Commodity-by-Commodity Total Requirement Matrix

These equations give total output of each commodity, expressed as a weighted sum of the commodity deliveries to final consumers (E_is). In deriving these equations, we assumed coefficients b_{ij}s and d_{ij}s are known. The set of weights written in matrix form is called the *commodity-by-commodity total requirement matrix*.

The ij element of the matrix gives the dollar value of the production of commodity i needed to meet the final demand of a dollar's worth of commodity j. The empirical illustration given above can be generalized, with matrix notations, as follows: If we denote by D the matrix whose ij element is d_{ij}, equation (16) can be generalized to

$$BDQ + E = Q$$

From this equation, it follows that

$$Q - BDQ = E, \text{ or}$$
$$(I - BD)Q = E,$$

yielding

$$Q = [(I - BD)^{-1}]\, E \qquad (19)$$

As mentioned above, each Q_j is expressed as a weighted sum of E_is. The weights are arranged in a matrix, whose form is the inverse of $(I - BD)$. In Table 8.4,

$$BD = \begin{pmatrix} (10/85) & (10/115) \\ (10/85) & (\ 4/115) \end{pmatrix} \begin{pmatrix} 0.85 & 0 \\ 0.15 & 1 \end{pmatrix} = \begin{pmatrix} 0.118 & 0.087 \\ 0.118 & 0.035 \end{pmatrix} \begin{pmatrix} 0.85 & 0 \\ 0.15 & 1 \end{pmatrix}$$

$$= \begin{pmatrix} 0.1130 & 0.0870 \\ 0.1052 & 0.0348 \end{pmatrix}$$

$$(I - BD) - 1 = \begin{pmatrix} 1.1396 & 0.1027 \\ 0.1242 & 1.0473 \end{pmatrix}$$

Consider again the analogous expression $(I - A)^{-1} = I + A + A^2 + \ldots$. It was mentioned earlier for the Leontief inverse in the traditional input–output model. Applying it, we have

$$(I - BD)^{-1} = I + BD + (BD)^2 + (BD)^3 + \ldots \qquad (20)$$

We may regard BD, on the right-hand side of equation (20), as the direct effect. The sum $(BD)^2 + (BD)^3 + \ldots$ represents the indirect effect. This usage follows the interpretation given earlier to A and $(A^2 + A^3 + \ldots)$, respectively, in connection with the Leontief inverse. It follows that the so-called constraints in the industry-by-commodity context can be represented as

$$(I - BD)^{-1} - I \qquad (21)$$

The corresponding numbers for the numerical example in Table 8.4 are

$$\begin{pmatrix} 0.1396 & 0.1027 \\ 0.1242 & 0.04732 \end{pmatrix}$$

Industry-by-Commodity Total Requirement Matrix

This matrix can be obtained by substituting for Q_j in equation (14) the weighted sum of E_is just mentioned. This gives an analogous weighted sum of E_is for each X_i. In matrix notation,

$$X = DQ = [D(I - BD)^{-1}]E$$

The quantity enclosed in brackets in this last equation is the industry-by-commodity total requirement matrix, giving the industry output required per dollar worth of each commodity delivered to final consumers.

Commodity-based Technology Assumptions. Let us define the *industry output proportions* as the commodity makeup of each industry. In our example, the commodity makeup of the two industries can be expressed as:

	Industry 1	Industry 2
Commodity 1	$c_{11} = v_{11}/X_1 = 85/85$	$c_{21} = v_{21}/X_2 = 15/115$
Commodity 2	$c_{12} = v_{12}/X_1 = 0/85$	$c_{22} = v_{22}/X_2 = 100/115$

The figures in the column under Industry 1 tell us that Industry 1 produces only Commodity 1. The figures in the next column show that Commodity 1 accounts for 13.04 percent of Industry 2's gross output, while the remaining is accounted for by Commodity 2. Assume that c_{ij}s remain time-invariant and that they apply no matter how large or small X_is are. Under these assumptions, and treating v_{ij}s and X_is as unspecified, we have the following for the particular illustrative case on hand:

$$v_{11} = c_{11}X_1 \qquad v_{21} = c_{21}X_2$$
$$v_{12} = c_{12}X_1 \qquad v_{22} = c_{22}X_2$$

But

$$v_{11} + v_{21} = Q_1 \text{ and } v_{12} + v_{22} = Q_2.$$

Substitution gives us this:

$$c_{11}X_1 + c_{21}X_2 = Q_1$$
$$c_{12}X_1 + c_{22}X_2 = Q_2$$

These equations predict Qs in terms of Xs, given c_{ij}s (the industry output proportions). In terms of the figures calculated above for c_{ij}s, the predicting equations are

$$X_1 + (15/115)X_2 = Q_1$$
$$(100/115)X_2 = Q_2$$

Expressing Xs in terms of Qs yields

$$X_1 = Q_1 - 0.15Q_2 \tag{22}$$
$$X_2 = 1.15Q_2$$

As mentioned before, equation (10) for the case here becomes

$$b_{11}X_1 + b_{12}X_2 + E_1 = Q_1$$
$$b_{21}X_1 + b_{22}X_2 + E_2 = Q_2$$

If we use b_{ij}s for the empirical values calculated earlier, the equivalent becomes

$$(10/85)X_1 + (10/115)X_2 + E_1 = Q_1$$
$$(10/85)X_1 + (\ 4/115)X_2 + E_2 = Q_2 \tag{23}$$

Substituting from equation (22) for the Xs in equation (23) yields

$$(10/85)(Q_1 - 0.15Q_2) + (10/115)1.15Q_2 + E_1 = Q_1$$
$$(10/85)(Q_1 - 0.15Q_2) + (\ 4/115)1.15Q_2 + E_2 = Q_2$$

or, on simplification,

$$(75/85)Q_1 - (7/85)Q_2 = E_1$$
$$-(10/85)Q_1 + (83.1/85)Q_2 = E_2$$

From this, we can obtain Q_is in terms of E_is:

$$Q_1 = 1.1462E_1 + 0.0966E_2 \tag{24}$$
$$Q_2 = 0.1379E_1 + 1.0345E_2$$

Total Commodity-by-Commodity Requirements

The equations in (24) are the total commodity-by-commodity requirements, based on the industry output proportions. They correspond to (but are different from) the total commodity-by-commodity requirements derived earlier using the commodity output proportions for an industry. From equation (24), obviously 0.1379 dollar's worth of Commodity 2 is required to deliver a dollar's worth of Commodity 1 to final demand.

REGIONAL INPUT–OUTPUT MODEL

Now suppose the necessary data are available for all commodities produced by producing organizations in each industry. The method for

Table 8.5
Flow-Data for a Hypothetical Two-Region Case

Selling Region/
 Sector   Purchasing Region/Sector

Region		Region 1 Sector:			Region 2 Sector:		Final Demand	Total Output*
	Sector:	1	2	3	1	2		
1	1	15	40	5	2	8	20	110
	2	20	10	40	20	10	100	210
	3	30	50	5	6	4	5	150
2	1	8	10	7	20	25	50	160
	2	5	2	3	15	10	45	100

*Includes deliveries to final demand

analyzing this information is analogous to methods used for regional input–output tables. An industry is treated analogously to a region. Just as each industry has multiple outputs, so does each region.

A Comparison of Two Hypothetical Regions

Consider the hypothetical data shown in Table 8.5. Two regions are represented, one having three sectors and the other two.
The regional input coefficients for Region 1 are:

	Sector 1	**Sector 2**	**Sector 3**
Sector 1	15/110	40/210	5/150
Sector 2	20/110	10/210	40/150
Sector 3	30/110	50/210	5/150

These are obtained by dividing the intraregional flows with the gross outputs. (The latter are the sum of intra- and interregional flows and deliveries to final demand.) Similarly, the regional input coefficients for Region 2 are:

	Sector 1	**Sector 2**
Sector 1	8/160	10/100
Sector 2	5/160	2/100

Interregional Trade Coefficients

The interregional trade coefficients from Region 1 to Region 2 are:

	Region 2: Sector 1	Region 2: Sector 2
Region 1		
Sector 1	2/160	8/100
Sector 2	20/160	10/100
Sector 3	6/160	4/100

Similarly, the interregional trade coefficients from Region 2 to Region 1 are:

	Region 1: Sector 1	Region 1: Sector 2	Region 1: Sector 3
Region 2			
Sector 1	8/110	10/210	7/150
Sector 2	5/110	2/210	3/150

These can be brought together in one rectangular arrangement, as shown below:

$$
A =
\begin{bmatrix}
15/110 & 40/210 & 5/150 & 2/160 & 8/100 \\
20/110 & 10/210 & 40/150 & 20/160 & 10/100 \\
30/110 & 50/210 & 5/150 & 6/160 & 4/100 \\
\hline
8/110 & 10/210 & 7/150 & 20/160 & 25/100 \\
5/110 & 2/210 & 3/150 & 15/160 & 10/100
\end{bmatrix}
$$

The entries are shown in fractions rather than decimally to bring out the mechanics of the calculations. Note that the flows in Table 8.5 are copied as such. Flows in column 1 are divided by the gross output in row 1 of Table 8.5. Those in column 2 are divided by the gross output in row 2, and so on. Stated in another way, the calculation of A proceeds as if the setup consists of an economy with five sectors.

The lines partition the matrix into four parts, as follows:

- The top-left submatrix displays the intraregional input coefficients of Region 1;
- The bottom-right submatrix displays the intraregional input coefficients of Region 2;
- The top-right submatrix displays the Region 1-to-Region 2 trade coefficients; and
- The bottom-left submatrix displays the Region 2-to-Region 1 trade coefficients.

For easy reference, let us attach to the top-left, top-right, bottom-left, and bottom-right submatrixes the labels $_1A_1$, $_1A_2$, $_2A_1$, and $_2A_2$, respectively. The Leontief inverse of A is

$$(I - A)^{-1} = \begin{bmatrix} 1.2785 & 0.5632 & 0.1816 & 0.1236 & 0.1599 \\ 0.2151 & 1.2390 & 0.2658 & 0.1722 & 0.1207 \\ 0.3469 & 0.5536 & 1.1699 & 0.1409 & 0.1164 \\ 0.1251 & 0.1671 & 0.1007 & 1.2080 & 0.2317 \\ 0.1082 & 0.1051 & 0.0718 & 0.2167 & 1.1652 \end{bmatrix}$$

Impacts from Changes in Final Demand

Impacts from various changes in final demand now can be calculated for sectors in each region, using the usual procedures. These impacts can be compared with the corresponding figures when Region 2 is merged with the environment of Region 1, thereby viewing Region 1 from the perspective of a single region. Note that when Region 2 is merged with the environment of Region 1, the input coefficients that we focus on are those in $_1A_1$, the top-left submatrix of A given above. The corresponding Leontief inverse is

$$(I - {_1A_1})^{-1} = \begin{bmatrix} 1.2553 & 0.5370 & 0.1648 \\ 0.1906 & 1.2093 & 0.2473 \\ 0.3254 & 0.5281 & 1.1538 \end{bmatrix}$$

The entries in the Leontief inverse of $_1A_1$ can be compared with the corresponding entries in the top-left submatrix of the Leontief inverse of A. This comparison reveals that the impact of an increase in final demand for the product of Region 1 is larger in the interregional setup (see the Leontief inverse of A) than in the single-region model (i.e., when Region 2 is merged with the environment of Region 1). The reason is that the former captures the interregional feedback, whereas the latter does not. Obviously, the difference between the two sets of figures will be small to the degree that Region 1 is self-sufficient. However, when Region 1 is dependent on import from or export to Region 2, the difference between the two sets of figures will be marked.

Implications

This last observation underscores the wisdom of explicitly incorporating the interdependence among organizations in one's model. The alternative of focusing on individual organizations one at a time, lumps all other organizations in a category called the environment. This focal organization approach obscures such differences.

CONCLUSIONS

The analysis of organizational networks has been plagued by a severe hiatus between theory and practice. It is commonly recognized that relationships among organizations are reciprocal, complex, and power-laden; yet, as we noted in Chapter 7, much of the research is preoccupied with one-way forms of dominance between dyads. We believe that the inconsistency is a natural product of the analytic techniques in vogue. Accordingly, we have proposed and illustrated an input–output model that is ideally suited to analyze relationships having the properties mentioned.

In the input–output model, the economy is viewed as divided into many segments or producing sectors. A sector may be an industry composed of producing organizations or any other aggregate of organizations, such as the firms in a geographic region. The basic data are the sector-to-sector flows of products as they move through the organizations that alternately produce and consume them. If each sector consists of organizations among whom no interdependence prevails, then the focus is on intersectoral flows of products. Otherwise, both intra- and intersectoral flows are of interest.

Confining attention to the simpler case in which the focus is on inter-sectoral flows, the input–output model assumes that, at least in the short run, the input mix or technology of production of outputs is time-invariant. This permits one to model the complete interdependent system of sectors as it responds to external demand for its outputs. The model involves the use of what is known as Leontief's inverse, which is a matrix of coefficients derived from the matrix of input coefficients.

This model of interdependence yields the following, among other things:

1. An explicit description of patterns of interdependence among organizations comprising industries, sectors, and regions.
2. A ranking of the sectors based on the power of each sector; power refers the total impact that a given investment would have on the system if that investment were made in one sector as opposed to the other sectors.
3. A clear picture of the direct and indirect effects on each sector that would occur from each dollar's worth of increased demand, compared to the output.
4. A delineation of all direct and indirect linkages among the various sectors, revealing two-way linkages wherever present.

Turning to the situation in which sectors are aggregates of interdependent entities like producing organizations, the appropriate input–output model is a modification of the traditional input–output model. The modified model in question is known as a regional input–output model. The analogy is between a region and a sector. A special feature of this model is that it pays attention to intraregional interdependence as well as interregional linkages. The impact of an increase in an externally originating investment or threat (e.g., of withdrawal of investment) in the regional input–output system is a function of both the intraregional and interregional linkages.

Any analysis that ignores the intraregional linkages when examining the response of the system to an external threat or investment is likely to yield biased results. Most of the world system analyses seem to have ignored this important principle. The same point applies to analyses in which attention is confined to interblock relationships, where blocks are aggregates of actors identified by means of block-modeling or other clustering procedures.

Bibliography

Abel, Theodore. "The Operation Called Verstechen." In Herbert Feigl and May Brodbeck, eds. *Readings in the Philosophy of Science* (pp. 677–687). New York: Appleton-Century-Crofts, 1953.

Aiken, Michael, and Jerald Hage. Organizational Interdependence and Intra-organizational Structure. *American Sociological Review* 33: 912–930, 1968.

Alba, Richard D. A Graph-Theoretic Definition of a Sociometric Clique. *Journal of Mathematical Sociology* 3: 113–126, 1973.

——. From Small Groups to Social Networks. *American Behavioral Science* 24: 681–694, 1981.

Aldrich, Howard E. *Organizations and Environments*. Englewood Cliffs, N.J.: Prentice-Hall, 1979.

Aldrich, Howard E., and David A. Whetten. "Organization-Sets, Action-Sets and Networks: Making the Most of Simplicity." In Paul C. Nystrom and William H. Starbuck, eds. *Handbook of Organizational Design: Adapting Organizations to Their Environments* (pp. 385–408), Vol 1. New York: Oxford University Press, 1981.

Aldrich, Howard, and Catherine Zimmer. "Entrepreneurship through Social Networks." In Donald Sexton and Raymond Smiler, eds. *The Art and Science of Entrepreneurship* (pp. 3–23). Cambridge, Mass.: Ballinger, 1986.

Alexander, Jeffrey C., and Bernhard Giesen. "From Reduction to Linkage: The Long View of the Micro-Macro Link." In J. C. Alexander, B. Giesen, R. Munch, and N. Smelser. eds. *The Micro-Macro Link* (pp. 1–44). Berkeley and Los Angeles: University of California Press, 1987.

Alexander, Karl L., Bruce K. Eckland, and Larry J. Griffin. The Wisconsin Model of Socioeconomic Achievement: A Replication. *American Journal of Sociology* 81: 324–342, 1981.

Astley, W. Graham. The Two Ecologies: Population and Community Perspectives on Organizational Evolution. *Administrative Science Quarterly* 30: 224–241, 1985.

Atkinson, A. B. *The Economics of Inequality*. Oxford: Clarendon Press, 1983.

Banfield, E. C. *The Unheavenly City*. Boston: Little, Brown, 1974.

Baron, James N., and William T. Bielby. The Organization of Work in a Segmented Economy. *American Sociological Review* 49: 454–473, 1984.

Baron, James N., and D. Strang. Categorical Imperatives: The Structure of Job Titles in California State Agencies. *American Sociological Review* 55: 479, 1990.

Beck, Lewis White. "Constructions and Inferred Entities." In Herbert Feigl and May Brodbeck, eds. *Readings in the Philosophy of Science* (pp. 368–381). New York: Appleton-Century-Crofts, 1953.

Becker, Gary S. *Human Capital.* New York: Columbia University Press for the National Bureau of Economic Research, 1964.

Benson, Kenneth. The Interorganizational Network as a Political Economy. *Administrative Science Quarterly.* 229–249, 1975.

Berger, Joseph, Dana P. Eyre, and Morris Zelditch, Jr. "Theoretical Structures and the Micro-Macro Problem." In Joseph Berger, Morris Zelditch, Jr., and Bo Anderson, eds. *Sociological Theories in Progress: New Formulations* (pp. 11–32). Newbury Park, Calif.: Sage, 1989.

Bergmann, Gustav. *Philosophy of Science.* Madison: University of Wisconsin Press, 1957.

Berkowitz, S. D. "Markets and Market-Areas: Some Preliminary Formulations." In Barry Wellman and S. D. Berkowitz, eds. *Social Structures: A Network Approach* (pp. 261–303). Cambridge: Cambridge University Press, 1988.

Bidwell, Charles E., and John D. Kasarda. *The Organization and Its Ecosystem: A Theory of Structure in Organizations.* Monographs on Organizational Behavior and Industrial Relations, Vol. 2. Greenwich, Conn.: JAI Press, 1985.

Blau, Peter M. *On the Nature of Organizations.* New York: John Wiley & Sons, 1974.

Blau, Peter M., Terry C. Blum, and Joseph E. Schwartz. Heterogeneity and Intermarriage. *American Sociological Review* 47: 45–62, 1982.

Blau, Peter, and O. D. Duncan. *The American Occupational Structure.* New York: John Wiley & Sons, 1967.

Blau, Peter M., and Joseph E. Schwartz. *Crosscutting Social Circles: Testing a Macrostructural Theory of Intergroup Relations.* Orlando, Fla.: Academic Press, 1984.

Blin, J. M., and C. Cohen. Technological Similarity and Aggregation in Input–Output Systems: A Cluster-Analytic Approach. *Review of Economics and Statistics* 59: 82–91, 1977.

Bock, R. Darrel, ed. *Multilevel Analysis of Educational Data.* San Diego: Academic Press, 1989.

Borgatta, Edgar F., and Kyle Kercher. "Social Network Analysis." In Samuel Kotz and Norman L. Johnson, eds. *Encyclopedia of Statistical Sciences* (pp. 537–539), Vol. 8. New York: Wiley, 1988.

Boswell, Terry, and William Dixon. Dependency and Rebellion: A Cross-National Analysis. *American Sociological Review* 55: 540–559, 1990.

Boudon, Raymond. "The Individualistic Tradition in Sociology." In J. C. Alexander, B. Giesen, R. Munch, and N. Smelser, eds. *The Micro-Macro Link.* Berkeley and Los Angeles: University of California Press, 1987.

Bradshaw, York. Urbanization and Underdevelopment: A Global Study of Modernization, Urban Bias and Economic Dependency. *American Sociological Review* 52: 224–239, 1987.

Braithwaite, John M. White Collar Crime. In Ralph Turner and James Short, eds. *Annual Review of Sociology* 11: 1–25. Palo Alto, Calif.: Annual Reviews, 1985.

Breiger, R. L. "Structures of Economic Interdependence among Nations." In Peter M. Blau and Robert K. Merton, eds. *Continuities in Structural Inquiry* (pp. 353–380). Beverly Hills, Calif.: Sage, 1981.

Breiger, R. L. *Explorations in Structural Analysis: Dual and Multiple Networks of Social Interaction.* New York: Garland, 1991.

Britt, David, and Omer R. Galle. Industrial Conflict and Unionization. *Administrative Science Quarterly* 37: 46–57, 1972.

Brittain, Jack W., and Douglas R. Wholey. "Competition and Coexistence in Organizational Communities: Population Dynamics in Electronic Components Manufacturing." In Glenn R. Carroll, ed. *Ecological Models of Organizations* (pp. 195–222). Cambridge, Mass.: Ballinger, 1988.

Brodbeck, May. "Models, Meanings and Theories." In L. Gross, ed. *Symposium on Sociological Theory* (pp. 373–403). Evanston, Ill.: Row, Petersen, 1959.

Brodbeck, May, ed. "Methodological Individualism: Definition and Reduction." In *Readings in the Philosophy of the Social Sciences* (pp. 280–303). New York: Macmillan, 1968.

Brouillette, J., and E. L. Quarantelli. Types of Patterned Variation in Bureaucratic Adaptations to Organizational Stress. *Sociological Inquiry* 41: 39–45, 1971.

Burawoy, Michael. Between the Labor Process and the State: The Changing Face of Factory Regimes Under Advanced Capitalism. *American Sociological Review* 48: 587–605, 1983.

Burns, Tom, and G. M. Stalker. *The Management of Innovation.* New York: Barnes & Noble, 1961.

Burt, Ronald S. Positions in Multiple Network Systems. I. A General Conception of Stratification and Prestige in a System of Actors Cast as a Topology. *Social Forces* 56: 106–131, 1977.

——. Cohesion versus Structural Equivalence as a Basis for Network Subgroups. *Sociological Methods and Research* 7: 189–212, 1978.

——. *Corporate Profits and Cooptation: Networks of Market Constraints and Directorate Ties in the American Economy.* New York: Academic Press, 1983.

Burt, Ronald S., Kenneth P. Christman, and Harold C. Kilburn, Jr. Testing a Structural Theory of Corporate Cooptation. *American Sociological Review* 45: 821–841, 1980.

Burt, Ronald S., and Michael Minor, eds. *Applied Network Analysis: A Methodological Introduction.* Beverly Hills, Calif.: Sage, 1983.

Caplow, Theodore. *Principles of Organization.* New York: Harcourt, Brace, 1964.

Carroll, Glenn R., ed. "Organizational Ecology in Theoretical Perspective." In *Ecological Models of Organizations* (pp. 1–6). Cambridge, Mass.: Ballinger, 1988.

Cartwright, D., and F. Harary. Structural Balance: A Generalization of Heider's Theory. *Psychological Review* 63: 277–292, 1956.

Champernowne, D. G. A Model of Income Distribution. *Economic Journal* 53: 318–351, 1953.

Chapman, David, and M. Lowther. Teachers' Satisfaction with Teaching. *Journal of Educational Research* 75: 241–247, 1982.

Chiswick, B. R. *Income Inequality.* Columbia University Press for the National Bureau of Economic Research, 1974.

Clark, Burton R. Interorganizational Patterns in Education. *Administrative Science Quarterly* 10: 224–237, 1965.

Cohen, Morris R. "Reason in Social Science." In Herbert Feigl and May Brodbeck, eds. *Readings in the Philosophy of Science* (pp. 663–673). New York: Appleton-Century-Crofts, 1953.

Cole, Stephen. *The Unionization of Teachers.* New York: Praeger, 1967.

Coleman, James S. "Social Structure and a Theory of Action." In Peter Blau, ed. *Approaches to the Study of Social Structure* (pp. 76–93). New York: Free Press, 1975.

——. "Microfoundations and Macrosocial Behavior." In J. C. Alexander, B. Giesen, R. Munch, and N. Smelser, eds. *The Micro-Macro Link* (pp. 153–173). Berkeley and Los Angeles: University of California Press, 1987.

Coleman, James S., and T. Hoffer. *Public and Private High Schools.* New York: Basic Books, 1987.

Collins, Randall. "Micro-Translation as a Theory Building Strategy." In Karin D. Knorr-Cetina and A. V. Circourel, eds. *Advances in Social Theory and Methodology* (pp. 81–108). London: Routledge, 1981.

——. "Interaction Ritual Chains, Power and Property: The Micro-Macro Connection as an Empirically Based Theoretical Problem." In J. C. Alexander, B. Giesen, R. Munch, and N. Smelser, eds. *The Micro-Macro Link* (pp. 193–200). Berkeley and Los Angeles: University of California Press, 1987.

Cook, Karen S., and J. M. Whitmeyer. "Two Approaches to Social Structure: Exchange Theory and Network Analysis." In Judith Blake and John Hagen, eds. *Annual Review of Sociology* (pp. 109–127), Vol. 18. Palo Alto, Calif.: Annual Reviews, 1992.

Cook, Karen S., and Richard Emerson. "Exchange Networks and the Analysis of Complex Organizations." In Edward J. Lawler and Samuel B. Backarack, eds. *Research in the Sociology of Organizations* (pp. 1–30), Vol. 3. Greenwich, Conn.: JAI Press, 1984.

Cook, Karen, Richard Emerson, Mary Gilmore, and Tohio Yamagishi. The Distribution of Power in Exchange Networks. *American Journal of Sociology* 89: 275–305, 1983.

Corwin, Ronald. G. "Organizational Skills and the 'Deskilling' Hypothesis." In Kathryn Borman and Jane Reisman, eds. *Becoming a Worker* (pp. 221–243). Norwood, N.J.: Ablex, 1986.

——. *The Organization–Society Nexus: A Critical Review of Models and Metaphors.* Westport, Conn.: Greenwood Press, 1987.

Corwin, Ronald G., and Krishnan Namboodiri, eds. "Have Individuals Been Overemphasized in School-Effects Research?" *Sociology of Education and Socialization: Methodological Issues* (pp. 141–176), Vol 8. Greenwich, Conn.: JAI Press, 1989.

Corwin, Ronald G., and Theodore C. Wagenaar. Boundary Interaction between Service Organizations and Their Publics: A Study of Teacher–Parent Relationships. *Social Forces* 55: 471–492, 1976.

Craig, C., J. Rubery, R. Tarling, and F. Wilkinson. *Labour Market Structures, Industrial Organization and Low Pay.* Cambridge: Cambridge University Press, 1982.

Danet, Brenda. "Client–Organization Relationships." In Paul C. Nystrom and William H. Starbuck, eds. *Handbook of Organizational Design: Remodeling Organizations and Their Environment* (pp. 382–428), Vol. 2. New York: Oxford University Press, 1981.

Davie, R., N. Butler, and H. Goldstein. *From Birth to Seven: The Second Report of the National Child Development Study.* White Plains, N.Y.: Longman, 1972.

Davis, H. T. *The Analysis of Economic Time Series.* Bloomington: Ind.: Principia Press, 1941.

Delacroix, Jacques, and Charles Ragin. Modernizing Institutions, Mobilization and Third World Development: A Cross-National Study. *American Journal of Sociology* 86: 1311–1347, 1978.

Delacroix, Jacques, and Michael E. Solt. "Niche Formation and Foundings in the California Wine Industry, 1941–84." In Glenn R. Carroll, ed. *Ecological Models of Organizations* (pp. 53–70). Cambridge, Mass.: Ballinger, 1988.

DiMaggio, Paul J., and Walter W. Powell. The Iron Cage Revisited: Institutional Isomorphism and Collective Rationality in Organizational Fields. *American Sociological Review* 48: 147–160, 1983.

Doeringer, P. B., and M. J. Piore. *Internal Labor Markets and Manpower Analysis.* Lexington, Mass.: D. C. Heath, 1971.

Douty, H. M. Sources of Occupational Wage and Salary Rate Dispersions within Labor Markets. *Industrial and Labor Relations Review* 14: 67–74, 1961.

Dreeben, Robert. *On What Is Learned in School.* Reading, Mass.: Addison-Wesley, 1968.

Easterlin, R. A. "Relative Economic Status and the American Fertility Swing." In E. Sheldon, ed. *Family Economic Behavior: Problems and Prospects* (pp. 170–223). Philadelphia: Lippincott, 1973.

Emerson, Richard M. "Power-Dependence Relations." *American Sociological Review* 27: 31–40, 1962.

Evan, William M. "An Organization-Set Model of Interorganizational Relations." In Matthew Tuite, Roger Chisholm, and Michael Radnor, eds. *Interorganizational Decision Making* (pp. 181–200). Chicago: Aldine, 1972.

Featherman, David L., and Robert M. Hauser. *Opportunity and Change.* New York: Academic Press, 1978.

Feigl, Herbert. "The Mind-Body Problem in the Development of Logical Empiricism." In Herbert Feigl and May Brodbeck, eds. *Readings in the Philosophy of Science* (pp. 612–626). New York: Appleton-Century-Crofts, 1953.

Fishburn, P. C. Transitive Measurable Utility. *Journal of Economic Theory* 31: 293–317, 1983.

Fisher, R. A. The Use of Multiple Measurements in Taxonomic Problems. *An-*

nals of Eugenics 7: 179–188, 1936.

Freeman, John. Going to the Well: School District Administrative Intensity and Environmental Constraints. *Administrative Science Quarterly* 24: 119–133, 1979.

Freeman, John, and Michael T. Hannan. Niche Width and the Dynamics of Organizational Populations. *American Journal of Sociology* 88: 1116–1145, 1983.

Freeman, R. B. Unionism and the Dispersion of Wages. *Industrial and Labor Relations Review* 34: 3–34, 1980.

Galaskiewicz, Joseph. *Exchange Networks and Community Politics.* Beverly Hills, Calif.: Sage, 1979.

Galaskiewicz, J., and Peter Marsden. Interorganizational Resource Networks: Formal Patterns of Overlap. *Social Science Research* 7: 89–107, 1989.

Galaskiewicz, Joseph, and Stanley Wasserman. Change in Regional Corporate Network. *American Sociological Review* 46: 475–484, 1981.

Gibrat, R. *Les Inegalities \ Economiques.* Paris, Sirey: 1931.

Giddens, Anthony. *The Constitution of Society: Outline of the Theory of Structuration.* Berkeley and Los Angeles: University of California Press, 1984.

Gintis, H. Education, Technology, and Characteristics of Worker Productivity. *American Economic Review* 61: 268–278, 1971.

Goffman, Erving. The Interaction Order. (Presidential Address.) *American Sociological Review* 48: 1–17, 1983.

Granovetter, Mark S. The Strength of Weak Ties. *American Journal of Sociology* 78: 1360–1380, 1973.

Griffin, James. *Energy Input–Output Modeling.* Palo Alto, Calif.: Electric Power Research Institute, 1976.

Griffin, Larry J., Michael Wallace, and Beth A. Rubin. Capitalist Resistance to the Organization of Labor Before the New Deal: Why? How? Success? *American Sociological Review* 51: 147–167, 1986.

Guetzkow, Harold. "Relations among Organizations." In R. V. Bowers, ed. *Studies of Behavior in Organizations: A Research Symposium* (pp. 13–44). Athens: University of Georgia Press, 1966.

Hage, Jerald. *Theories of Organizations: Form, Process, and Transformations.* New York: Wiley Interscience, 1980.

Hall, Richard, John P. Clark, Peggy Gordano, Paul Johnson, and Martha Van Roekel. Patterns of Interorganizational Relationships. *Administrative Science Quarterly* 22: 457–474, 1977.

Hannan, Michael, and John Freeman. The Population Ecology of Organizations. *American Journal of Sociology* 82: 929–964, 1977.

——. Structural Inertia and Organizational Change. *American Sociological Review* 49: 149–164, 1984.

——. *Organizational Ecology.* Cambridge: Harvard University Press, 1989.

Hawley, Amos H. "Human Ecology." In J. F. Short, ed. *The State of Sociology: Problems and Prospects.* Beverly Hills, Calif.: Sage, 1981.

——. "The Logic of Macrosociology." In Judith Blake and John Hagen, eds. *Annual Review of Sociology* (pp. 1–14), Vol. 18. Palo Alto, Calif.: Annuals Reviews, 1992.

Hechter, Michael, ed. Introduction. In *The Microfoundations of Macrosociology* (pp. 3–15). Philadelphia: Temple University Press, 1983.

Hechter, Michael, ed. "A Theory of Group Solidarity." In *The Microfoundations of Macrosociology* (pp. 16–57). Philadelphia: Temple University Press, 1983.

Hempel, C. G., and P. Oppenheim. "The Logic of Explanation." In Herbert Feigl and May Brodbeck, eds. *Readings in the Philosophy of Science* (pp. 319–352). New York: Appleton-Century-Crofts, 1953.

Hermalin, A. I., and W. M. Mason. "A Strategy for the Comparative Analysis of WFS Data, with Illustrative Examples." In *The United Nations Program for Comparative Analysis of World Fertility Survey Data* (pp. 90–168). New York: United Nations Fund for Population Activities, 1980.

Higley, John, and Michael Burton. The Elite Variable in Democratic Transitions and Breakdowns. *American Sociological Review* 54: 17–32, 1989.

Hirsch, Paul M. Organizational Effectiveness and the Institutional Environment. *Administrative Science Quarterly* 20: 327–344, 1975.

Hodson, Randy. Companies, Industries, and the Measurement of Economic Size. *American Sociological Review* 49: 335–348, 1984.

Hodson, Randy, and Robert L. Kaufman. Economic Dualism: A Critical Review. *American Sociological Review* 47: 727–739, 1982.

Hunter, L. C., and D. J. Robertson. *Economics of Wages and Labour*. London: Macmillan, 1969.

Huntington, Samuel P. *Political Order in Changing Societies*. New Haven: Yale University Press, 1968.

Jenkins, J. Craig. "Resource Mobilization Theory and the Study of Social Movements." In Ralph Turner and James F. Short, eds. *Annual Review of Sociology* (pp. 527–553), Vol. 9. Palo Alto, Calif.: Annual Reviews, 1983.

Kadushin, Charles. Notes on Expectations of Reward in N-Person Networks. In Peter M. Blau and Robert K. Merton, eds. *Continuities in Structural Inquiry* (pp. 235–254). Beverly Hills, Calif.: Sage, 1981.

Kerckhoff, Alan. "The Status Attainment Process: Socialization or Allocation?" *Social Forces* 55: 368–381, 1976.

Kimberly, John R. Organization Size and the Structuralist Perspective: A Review, Critique and Proposal. *Administrative Science Quarterly* 21: 577–597, 1976.

Klatzky, Sheila. The Relationship of Organizational Size to Complexity and Coordination. *Administrative Science Quarterly* 15: 528–538, 1970.

Knoke, David. *Collective Action: The Political Economies of Associations*. Hawthorne, N.Y.: A. de Gruyter, 1990.

Knoke, David, and James H. Kuklinski. *Network Analysis*. Beverly Hills, Calif.: Sage, 1982.

Lammers, Cornelis J. Strikes and Mutinies: A Comparative Study of Organizational Conflicts Between Rulers and Ruled. *Administrative Science Quarterly* 14: 558–572, 1969.

Larson, Andrea. "Partner Networks: Leveraging External Ties to Improve Entrepreneurial Performance." *Journal of Business Venturing* 6: 173–188, 1991.

——. Network Dyads in Entrepreneurial Settings: A Study of the Governance of Exchange Processes. *Administrative Science Quarterly* 37: 76–104, 1992.

Laumann, Edward O., and David Knoke. *The Organizational State: Social*

Choice in National Policy Domains. Madison: University of Wisconsin Press, 1987.

Laumann, Edward O., Joseph Galaskiewicz, and Peter Marsden. Community Structures as Interorganization Linkages. In Ralph H. Turner, James Coleman, and Renee Fox, eds. *Annual Review of Sociology* 4: 455–484. Palo Alto, Calif.: Annual Reviews, 1978.

Lawrence, Paul R., and Jay W. Lorsch. Differentiation and Integration in Complex Organizations. *Administrative Science Quarterly* 12: 1–47, 1967.

Lazarsfeld, Paul S., and Herbert Menzel. "On the Relationship between Individual and Collective Properties." In Amitai Etzioni, ed. *Complex Organizations: A Sociological Reader* (pp. 422–440). New York: Holt, Rinehart Winston, 1961.

Lazarsfeld, Paul S., and Wagner Thielens. *The Academic Mind.* New York: Free Press, 1958.

Leifer, Eric M., and Harrison C. White. A Structural Approach to Markets. In Mark S. Mizruchi and Michael Schwartz, eds. *Intercorporate Relations: The Structural Analysis of Business* (pp. 85–108). Cambridge: Harvard University Press, 1987.

Levine, Sol, and Paul E. White. Exchange as a Conceptual Framework for the Study of Interorganizational Relationships. *Administrative Science Quarterly* 5: 583–601, 1961.

Levine, Sol, Paul E. White, and Benjamin D. Paul. Community Interorganizational Problems in Providing Medical Care and Social Services. *American Journal of Public Health* 53: 1183–1195, 1963.

Lewis, H. G. *Unionism and Relative Wages in the United States.* Chicago: University of Chicago Press, 1963.

Lieberson, Stanley. *A Piece of the Pie: Blacks and White Immigrants since 1880.* Berkeley and Los Angeles: University of California Press, 1980.

Litwak, Eugene, and Lydia F. Hylton. Interoganizational Analysis: A Hypothesis on Coordinating Agencies. *Administrative Science Quarterly* 6: 31–58, 1962.

Lortie, Dan C. *School Teacher: A Sociological Study.* Chicago: University of Chicago Press, 1975.

Lutz, M. A. The Evolution of the Industrial Earnings Structure: The Geological Theory. *Canadian Journal of Economics* 9: 473–491, 1976.

Lyndall, Harold. *A Theory of Income Distribution.* Oxford: Clarendon Press, 1979.

Lyndall, H. F. *The Structure of Earnings.* New York: Oxford University Press, 1968.

McCarthy, John D., Mark Wolfson, David Baker, and Elaine Mosakowski. The Founding of Social Movement Organizations: Local Citizens' Groups Opposing Drunken Driving. In Glenn R. Carroll, ed., *Ecological Models of Organization* (pp. 71–84). Cambridge, Mass.: Ballinger, 1988.

McEachern, William A. *Managerial Control and Performance.* Lexington, Mass.: D. C. Heath, 1975.

Mandelbrot, B. "The Pareto-Levy Law and the Distribution of Income." *International Economic Review* 1: 79–106, 1960.

Marx, Karl. *Das Capital.* Moscow: Foreign Languages Publishing House, 1954.

Mason, W. M., G. W. Wong, and B. Entwisle. "Contextual Analysis through the Multilevel Linear Model." In S. Leinhardt, ed. *Sociological Method-*

ology 1983–1984 (pp. 72–103). San Francisco: Jossey-Bass, 1983.

Mayhew, Bruce H. Structuralism versus Individualism. I. Shadowboxing in the Dark. *Social Forces* 59: 335–375, 1980.

——. Structuralism versus Individualism. II. Ideological Obfuscations. *Social Forces* 60: 627–648, 1981.

Meyer, Marshall. *Bureaucratic Structure and Authority.* New York: Harper & Row, 1972.

——. *Change in Public Bureaucracies.* Cambridge: Cambridge University Press, 1979.

Miles, Raymond E., and Kim S. Cameron. *Coffin Nails and Corporate Strategy.* Englewood Cliffs, N.J.: Prentice-Hall, 1982.

Miller, Ronald E., and Peter D. Blair. *Input–Output Analysis: Foundations and Extensions.* Englewood Cliffs, N.J.: Prentice-Hall, 1985.

Mincer, J. The Distribution of Labor Incomes: A Survey. *Journal of Economic Literature* 8: 1–26, 1970.

——. *Schooling, Experience, and Earnings.* New York: Columbia University Press, 1974.

——. "Progress in Human Capital Analysis of the Distribution of Earnings." In A. B. Atkinson, ed. *The Personal Distribution of Incomes.* Allen & Unwin, 1976.

——. Human Capital and Earnings. In A. B. Atkinson, ed. *Wealth, Income and Inequality* (pp. 103–128). New York: Oxford University Press, 1980.

Miyazawa, K. *Lecture Notes in Economics and Mathematical Systems: Input–Output Analysis and the Structure of Income Distribution.* Heidelberg: Springer-Verlag, 1976.

Mizruchi, Mark S. *The American Corporate Network, 1904–1974.* Beverly Hills, Calif.: Sage, 1982.

——. Similarity of Political Behavior among Large American Corporations. *American Journal of Sociology* 95: 401–424, 1989.

——. *The Structure of Corporate Political Action: Interfirm Relations and Their Consequences.* Cambridge: Harvard University Press, 1991.

Mulvey, C. Collective Agreements and Relative Earnings in U.K. Manufacturing in 1973. *Economics* 43: 419ff., 1976.

Mulvey, C., and J. M. Abowd. Estimating the Union/Non-Union Wage Differential: A Statistical Issue. *Economics* 47: 73–85, 1980.

Nagel, Ernest. On the Method of *Verstehen* as the Sole Method of Philosophy. *The Journal of Philosophy* 1: 154–157, 1953.

Namboodiri, Krishnan. Ecological Demography: Its Place in Sociology. *American Sociological Review* 53: 619–633, 1988.

Ord, J. K. "Statistical Models for Personal Income Distribution." In G. P. Patil, S. Kotz, and J. K. Ord, eds. *Statistical Distributions in Scientific Work* (pp. 151–158), Vol. 2. Boston: D. Reidel, 1975.

Ornstein, Michael. Interlocking Directorates in Canada: Intercorporate or Class Alliance? *Administrative Science Quarterly* 29: 210–231, 1984.

Palmer, Donald A., and Roger Friedland. "Corporation, Class, and City System." In Mark S. Mizruchi and Michael Schwartz, eds. *Intercorporate Relations: The Structural Analysis of Business* (pp. 145–184). Cambridge, U.K.: Cambridge University Press, 1987.

Parcel, Toby L., and M. Sickmeier. One Firm, Two Labor Markets: The Case of

McDonald's in the Fast Food Industry. *Sociological Quarterly* 29: 29–46, 1988.

Parsons, Talcott. *Structure and Process in Modern Societies*. Glencoe, Ill.: Free Press, 1960.

Parsons, Talcott, ed. *Max Weber: The Theory of Social and Economic Organization*. New York: Free Press, 1947.

Pennings, Johannes M. *Interlocking Directorates*. San Francisco: Jossey-Bass, 1980.

———. "Strategically Interdependent Organizations." In P. C. Nystrom and W. H. Starbuck, eds. *Handbook of Organizational Design: Adapting Organizations to Their Environments* (pp. 433–455), Vol. 2. New York: Oxford University Press, 1981.

Perrone, Luca. Positional Power, Strikes, and Wages. In Erik Olin Wright and Larry J. Griffin, eds. *American Sociological Review* 49: 412–426, 1984.

Perrucci, Robert, and Marc Pilisuk. Leaders and Ruling Elites: The Interorganizational Bases of Community Power. *American Sociological Review* 35: 1040–1056, 1970.

Pfeffer, Jeffrey. *Organizations and Organization Theory*. Boston: Pitman, 1982.

———. "A Resource Dependence Perspective on Intercorporate Relations." In Mark S. Mizruchi, and Michael Schwartz, eds. *Intercorporate Relations: The Structural Analysis of Business* (pp. 25–55). Cambridge: Cambridge University Press, 1987.

Pfeffer, Jeffrey, and Gerald R. Salancik. *The External Control of Organizations*. New York: Harper & Row, 1978.

Phelps Brown, E. H. *The Economics of Labor*. New Haven: Yale University Press, 1962.

———. *The Inequality of Pay*. Oxford: The University Press, 1977.

Powell, Walter. "Neither Market nor Hierarchy: Network Forms of Organization." In Barry M. Straw and L. L. Cummings, eds. *Research in Organization Behavior* (pp. 295–336), Vol. 12. Greenwich Conn.: JAI Press, 1990.

Psacharopoulos, G. *Earnings and Education in OECD Countries*. Paris: O.E.C.D., 1975.

Rees, A., and G. Schultz. *Workers and Wages in an Urban Labor Market*. Chicago: University of Chicago Press, 1970.

Richardson, Harry W. *Input–Output and Regional Economics*. New York: Wiley (Halsted Press), 1972.

Robinson, Robert V., and Jonathan Kelley. Class as Conceived by Marx and Dahrendorf: Effects on Income Inequality and Politics in the United States and Great Britain. *American Sociological Review* 44: 38–58, 1979.

Ryle, Gilbert. *The Concept of Mind*. London: Hutchinson, 1949.

Schmidt, Stuart M., and Thomas A. Kochan. Conflict: Toward Conceptual Clarity. *Administrative Science Quarterly* 17: 359–370, 1972.

Segal, M. Organization and Environment – A Typology of Adaptability and Structure. *Public Administration Review* 34: 212–220, 1974.

Selznick, Philip. Foundations of the Theory of Organizations. *American Sociological Review* 13: 25–35, 1948.

———. *TVA and the Grass Roots*. Berkeley and Los Angeles: University of California Press, 1949.

Sewell, William H., and Robert H. Hauser. *Education, Occupation, and Earnings: Achievement in the Early Career.* New York: Academic Press, 1975.

Shorter, Edward, and Charles Tilly. *Strikes in France: 1830–1968.* Cambridge: Cambridge University Press, 1974.

Sieber, Sam D. *Fatal Remedies: The Ironies of Social Intervention.* New York: Plenum, 1981.

Simmel, Georg. *The Sociology of Georg Simmel.* Trans. K. Wolff. Glencoe, Ill.: Free Press, 1950.

Simon, H. A. The Compensation of Executives. *Sociometry* 20: 32–41, 1957.

Singh, S. K., and G. S. Maddala. A Function for Size Distribution of Incomes. *Econometrica* 44: 963–970, 1976.

Smith, Catherine Begniche. Influence of Internal Opportunity Structure and Sex of Workers on Turnover Patterns. *Administrative Science Quarterly* 24: 362–381, 1979.

Smith, David, and Douglas R. White. Structure and Dynamics of the Global Economy: Network Analysis of International Trade 1965-1980. *Social Forces* 70: 857–893, 1992.

Snyder, D., and E. L. Kick. Structural Position in the World System and Economic Growth, 1955-1970: A Multiple-Network Analysis of Transnational Interactions. *American Journal of Sociology* 84: 1046–1126, 1979.

Snyder, David, and Charles Tilly. Hardship and Collective Violence in France 1830 to 1960. *American Sociological Review* 37: 520–532, 1972.

Sommerhoff, G. *Analytical Biology.* New York: Oxford University Press, 1950.

Sorenson, Aage B., and Arne L. Kallenberg. "An Outline of a Theory of the Matching of Persons to Jobs." In Ivar Berg, ed. *Sociological Perspectives on Labor Markets* (pp. 49–78). New York: Academic Press, 1981.

Spaeth, Joe L. Job Power and Earnings. *American Sociological Review* 50: 603–617, 1985.

Spilerman, Seymour. Careers, Labor Market Structure, and Socioeconomic Achievement. *American Journal of Sociology* 83: 551–593, 1977.

Starr, Paul. *The Social Transformation of American Medicine.* New York: Basic Books, 1982.

Stewman, Shelby, and Suresh Konda. Careers and Organizational Labor Markets: Demographic Models of Organizational Behavior. *American Journal of Sociology* 88: 637–685, 1983.

Stinchcombe, Arthur L. Bureaucratic and Craft Administration of Production: A Comparative Study. *Administrative Science Quarterly* 4: 168–187, 1959.

Stolzenberg, Ross M. Bringing the Boss Back In. *American Sociological Review* 43: 813–828, 1978.

Terreberry, Shirley. The Evolution of Administrative Environments. *Administrative Science Quarterly* 12: 590–618, 1968.

Thompson, James D. *Organizations in Action.* New York: McGraw-Hill, 1967.

Thompson, James D., and William McEwen. Organizational Goals and Environment: Goal Setting as an Interaction Process. *American Sociological Review* 23: 23–31, 1958.

Thurow, L. C. *Generating Inequality.* London: Macmillan, 1976.

Thurow, L. C., and R. E. B. Lucas. *The American Distribution of Income: A Structural Problem.* Washington, D.C.: U.S. Government Printing Office, 1972.

Tinbergen, J. *Income Distribution: Analysis and Policies*. Amsterdam, North-Holland: 1975.

Turk, Herman. *Organizations in Modern Life*. San Francisco: Jossey-Bass, 1977.

Turner, Merele B. *Philosophy and the Science of Behavior*. New York: Appleton-Century-Crofts, 1965.

Useem, Michael. *The Inner Circle: Large Corporations and the Rise of Business Political Activity in the U.S. and the U.K.* New York: Oxford University Press, 1984.

Wachtel, H. M., and C. Betsy. Employment at Low Wages. *Review of Economics and Statistics* 54: 121–132, 1972.

Warner, W. Lloyd, Robert J. Havighurst, and Martin B. Loeb. *Who Shall Be Educated? The Challenge of Unequal Opportunities*. New York: Harper & Brothers, 1948.

Warren, Roland. The Interorganizational Field as a Focus for Investigation. *Administrative Science Quarterly* 12: 396–419, 1967.

Warren, Roland, Stephen Rose, and Ann Bergunder. *The Structure of Urban Reform*. Lexington, Mass.: D. C. Heath, 1974.

Watkins, J. W. N. "Ideal Types and Historical Explanation." In Herbert Feigl and May Brodbeck, eds. *Readings in the Philosophy of Science* (pp. 723–743). New York: Appleton-Century-Crofts, 1953.

Wayland, Sloan. "Structural Features of American Education as Basic Factors in Innovation." In Mathew Miles, ed. *Innovation in Education* (pp. 587–613). New York: Teachers College Press, 1963.

Webb, S., and B. Webb. *Industrial Democracy*. London: Longman's Green, 1902.

Webster, Murray. Psychological Reductionsim, Methodological Individualism, and Large Scale Problems. *American Sociological Reveiw* 38: 258–273, 1973.

Weidenbaum, Murray L. *Business, Government, and the Public*. Englewood Cliffs, N.J.: Prentice-Hall, 1977.

Weiss, L. Concentration of Labor Earnings. *American Economic Review* 56: 96–117, 1966.

Wellman, Barry. "Structural Analysis: From Method and Metaphore to Theory and Substance." In Barry Wellman and S. D. Berkowitz, eds. *Social Structures: A Network Approach* (pp. 19–61). Cambridge: Cambridge University Press, 1988.

White, Harrison C. Management Conflict and Sociometric Structure. *American Journal of Sociology* 67: 185–199, 1961.

——. *Chains of Opportunity: System Models of Mobility in Organizations*. Cambridge: Harvard University Press, 1970.

White, Harrison C., Scott A. Boorman, and Ronald L. Breiger. Social Structure from Multiple Networks. I. Blockmodels of Roles and Positions. *American Journal of Sociology* 81: 730–780, 1976.

Whitt, J. Allen. Means of Movement: The Political Economy of Mass Transportation. In Michael Schwartz, ed. *The Structure of Power in America: The Corporate Elite as a Ruling Class* (pp. 123–135). New York: Holmes and Meier, 1987.

Wiewel, William, and Albert Hunter. The Interorganizational Network as a Resource: A Comparative Case Study of Organizational Genesis. *Administrative Science Quarterly* 30: 482–496, 1985.

Wilensky, Harold. "Work, Careers, and Social Integration." *International Social Science Journal* 12: 543–560, 1960.

Wong, G. Y., and W. M. Mason. The Hierarchical Logistic Regression Model for Multilevel Analysis. *Journal of the American Statistical Association* 80: 513–524, 1985.

Wright, Erik Olin. "Postscript." In Luca Perrone. Positional Power, Strikes, and Wages. *American Sociological Review* 49: 421–426, 1984.

Wright, Erik Olin, and Luca Perrone. Marxist Class Categories and Income Inequality. *American Sociological Review* 42: 32–55, 1977.

Young, Ruth. Is Population Ecology a Useful Paradigm for the Study of Organizations? *American Journal of Sociology* 94: 1–24, 1988.

Zald, Mayer N. *Organizational Change: The Political Economy of the Y.M.C.A.* Chicago: University of Chicago Press, 1970.

Zammuto, Raymond F., and Kim S. Cameron. "Environmental Decline and Organizational Response." In Larry L. Cummings and Barry M. Straw, eds. *Research in Organizational Behavior* (pp. 223–262), Vol. 7. Greenwich, Conn.: JAI Press, 1985.

Zander, M. Welfare Reform and the Uban Aged. *Society* 15: 59–67, 1978.

Zimmermann, Ekkart. "Macro-Comparative Research on Political Protest." In Ted R. Gurr, ed. *Handbook of Political Conflict: Theories and Research* (pp. 167–237). New York: Free Press, 1980.

Zucker, Lynne G. Combining Institutional Theory and Population Ecology: No Legitimacy, No History. *American Sociological Review* 54: 542–545, 1989.

Author Index

Lewis, H.G., 93, 148
Lieberson, S., 94, 148
Litwak, E., 69, 148
Loeb, M.B., 82, 152
Lorsch, J.W., 35, 148
Lortie, D.C., 91, 148
Lowther, M., 92, 144
Lucas, R.E.B., 89, 151
Lutz, M.A., 93, 148
Lyndall, H.F., 74, 78, 80, 81, 83, 84, 89, 148

McCarthy, J.D., 38, 148
McEachern, W.A., 108, 148
McEwen, S.P., 42, 151
Maddala, G.S., 86, 151
Mandelbrot, B., 86, 148
Markov, A.A., 110
Marsden, P.V., 119, 146, 148
Marx, K., 25, 88, 148
Mason, W.M., 16, 147, 148, 152
Mayhew, B.H., 3, 6, 149
Menzel, H., 5, 11, 13, 22, 24, 148
Meyer, M., 69, 149
Miles, R.E., 40, 149
Miller, R.E., 119, 130, 149
Mincer, J., 74, 77, 78, 149
Minor, M., 143
Miyazawa, K., 100, 149
Mizruchi, M.S., 57, 107, 149
Mosakowski, E., 38, 148
Mulvey, C., 93, 149

Nagel, E., 5, 149
Namboodiri, K., 24, 25, 32, 41, 42, 80, 81, 82, 144, 149

Oppenheim, P., 5, 6, 147
Ord, J.K., 86, 149
Ornstein, M., 57, 149

Palmer, D.A., 30, 149
Parcel, T.L., 96, 149
Pareto, W., 85, 86
Parsons, T., 5, 24, 150
Paul, B.D., 69, 148
Pennings, J.M., 56, 57, 119, 150
Perrone, L., 27, 60, 89, 150

Perrucci, R., 57, 150
Pfeffer, J., 36, 57, 68, 105, 106, 107, 109, 110, 150
Phelps Brown, E.H., 80, 93, 150
Pilisuk, M., 57, 150
Piore, M.J., 90, 93, 96, 104, 145
Powell, W.W., 36, 46, 108, 145, 150
Psacharopoulos, G., 81, 150

Quarantelli, E.L., 36, 143

Ragin, C.C., 28, 145
Rees, A., 87, 150
Richardson, H.W., 119, 150
Robertson, D.J., 92, 147
Robinson, R.V., 89, 150
Rose, S., 62, 152
Rubery, J., 145
Rubin, B.A., 27, 146
Ryle, G., 5, 150

Salancik, G.R., 57, 110, 150
Schmidt, S.M., 62, 150
Schultz, G., 87, 150
Schwartz, J.E., 26, 142
Segal, M., 68, 150
Selznick, P., 57, 150
Sewell, W.H., 81, 151
Shorter, E., 27, 151
Sickmeier, M., 96, 149
Sieber, S.D., 8, 151
Simmel, G., 3, 151
Simon, H.A., 89, 151
Singh, S.K., 86, 151
Smith, A., 75
Smith, C.B., 96, 151
Smith, D., 113, 114, 151
Snyder, D., 27, 113, 151
Solt, M.E., 38, 145
Sommerhoff, G., 10, 151
Sorenson, A.B., 90, 103, 151
Spaeth, J.L., 89, 151
Spilerman, S., 91, 104, 151
Stalker, G.M., 36, 143, 151
Starr, P., 37, 151
Stewman, S., 88, 91, 151
Stinchcombe, A., 35, 151
Stolzenberg, R.M., 96, 151

Subject Index

ABOUT THE AUTHORS

KRISHNAN NAMBOODIRI is Professor and Chair of the Department of Sociology at Ohio State University. He has published extensively in sociology.

RONALD G. CORWIN is Professor of Sociology at Ohio State University. He is the author, co-author, or editor of several books, including *The Organization-Society Nexus* (Greenwood Press, 1987).